JOAN OF ARC

WILLIAM TELL

Schiller

VOLUME THREE

Joan of Arc
William Tell

TRANSLATED BY
ROBERT DAVID MACDONALD

OBERON BOOKS
LONDON

WWW.OBERONBOOKS.COM

This translation of *Joan of Arc* first published in 1987 by
Oberon Books Ltd
This translation of *William Tell* first published in 2005 by
Oberon Books Ltd
521 Caledonian Road, London, N7 9RH
Tel: 020 7607 3637 / Fax: 020 7607 3629
e-mail: info@oberonbooks.com
www.oberonbooks.com

Joan of Arc published in single-volume edition, 1998

New three-volume edition, 2005

A catalogue record for this book is available from the
British Library.

PB ISBN: 9781840026207

Woodcut illustrations by Andrzej Klimowski

Contents

Introduction

by Nicholas Dromgoole

JOAN OF ARC was written in 1801. As with *Mary Stuart*, written a year earlier, an English audience cannot be entirely impartial. Some of our historical sympathies are inevitably involved in a depressingly chauvinistic way. The English burnt Joan of Arc as a witch. The French still worship her as a saint. Does a flavour of these ancient antipathies still linger?

Nothing could better emphasise the extraordinary difference that Romanticism effected in our culture than Schiller's choice of subject matter for this play. Voltaire, that embodiment of *raison et lumière* had demolished Joan of Arc in a long and scabrously amusing poem, *La Pucelle.* As a result the saintly Joan of Arc was – and had been for some time – entirely exploded, a mere figure of fun. It is difficult for us to realise how boldly Schiller set about rehabilitating her. We are almost edging into the lurid territory of Victor Hugo's *Notre-Dame de Paris* (*The Hunchback of Notre-Dame*). Religion, sentimentality, the oddly bizarre and the romantic past all jumbled up to tear at our heart strings.

Once again Schiller reorganised the facts with scant regard for accuracy. In his play, Joan of Arc is not burnt at all, but perishes in fine style on the battlefield. Far from being the modest creation of Bernard Shaw or Max Mell's *Jeanne d'Arc,* Schiller's Joan has high-flown rhetoric in abundance. Even more interesting is the way she see-saws between having a powerful sense of destiny, and losing her authority from a sense of guilt. Indeed in Schiller's play she verges on the manic-depressive, bouts of exultation followed by despair.

In *Mary Stuart,* Mary knew she was innocent of the Babington plot, but felt guilty about her part in her young husband's murder years before. She only regained her confidence when faced with the death sentence. Guilt gnawed at her sense of justice and authority. How could Right be on her side when she herself had done such wrongs?

This theme of guilt was continued in *Joan of Arc.* Joan, when faced by an English knight, Lionel, fights him in single combat and defeats him, but touched by love and pity, spares his life. This leaves her with a strong sense of guilt, of having failed in her divine mission and surrendered to earthly passion. When her father denounced her publicly as a witch in the play, she was too conscious of this feeling of guilt to rebut the charges, did not defend herself and was banished. Wandering in the forest – how many romantic heroines have not wandered in the forest? – she was of course captured by Lionel's guard and then resisted his physical advances.

Having rejected him she then see-saws up to a state of exultation again which allows her to escape, and rescue the King. She then wins the battle and dies gloriously draped with banners on the battlefield.

Why does guilt play such a part in these later plays? Did Schiller himself equate a sense of guilt with the loss of power, of authority, of creativity? Did he himself harbour feelings of guilt? Few dramatists of his power and authority have written nothing for the theatre for a decade, almost a half of his adult life.

Of course, Romanticism and guilt were almost irreconcilable concepts. Romanticism, based on a wishy-washy belief that everybody is basically good, cannot cope with guilt. Redemption was always just around the corner, a happy ending part of the territory. So Schiller was flirting with the unacceptable, but only flirting. In a dramatic sense *Joan of Arc* does have a happy ending. Joan has overcome the self-doubt and divisions in her own nature and finally achieved her true destiny. Schiller's heroes and heroines reach the sublime in the grand way they use their conscious wills to submit to a destiny that is unavoidable. To re-write Shakespeare, 'the submission is all'.

Schiller was a sick man by the time he came to write *Joan of Arc,* but two further successful plays lay ahead: *The Bride of Messina* and *William Tell.* It is generally accepted that *William Tell* was his best play. The writing of it was not made easier by the descent upon Weimar of that indefatigable culture-vulture, Madame de Staël, a French émigré and opponent of Napoleon, and an early example of those publicity-conscious individuals who can cleverly manipulate public opinion. She had in her own time an extraordinary influence on the thinking of educated Europeans. She sat firmly in Weimar and talked at length to Goethe and Schiller about the Divinity, about creation, about philosophy and about literature. When the many long weeks of her visit were over, Schiller told a friend that he felt it was like the end of a long and painful illness. All the same her subsequent book, *De l'Allemagne*, did much to establish Germany as a new and important centre in European thought and culture, and inspired both Carlyle and Coleridge, among others, to learn German. In spite of this draining experience, Schiller still managed to work away at *William Tell* whenever he could. Its emphasis on freedom may have had a private resonance for him, which only Goethe, equally victimised by de Staël, may have fervently shared.

The legend of William Tell belongs to the fourteenth century, with both the shooting of the apple on his son's head, and the near miraculous escape from Gessler's barge. Agidius Tschudi (1505–72), in his best known work, *Chronikon Helveticum* – which covered the period 1000 to 1470, and was published in 1734–6 – was the earliest historian to set out the story of William Tell as we still know it, and this source was used by Schiller as the basis for his play. Its authenticity was seriously questioned later in the century, but, as with Robin Hood and Sherwood Forest, who cares about authenticity when the legend is already so firmly a part of folklore? If it did not really happen like that it certainly should have!

Strictly speaking, *William Tell* is not a tragedy, but a *Schauspiel*, a term used since the end of the 18th century to describe a serious play which did not end with the death of its hero or broke the strict rules of French classical tragedy. William Tell lives on at the end of the play, which bears little resemblance to any example of French classicism. Indeed, in the first act, Schiller is positively Shakespearian in the brilliantly skilful way he brings unity to a varied collection of scattered events which taken together give a vivid picture of Austrian oppression over the Swiss. Schiller had never been to Switzerland, and relied on Goethe who had done so, but the Alps, the mountain lakes, the dawn over wooded slopes, the valiant Swiss people's lives and feelings all come to life in the play. In a review, Schiller had written of the difficulty of achieving a popular style. 'What a task it is to please the demanding taste of the gifted few, without losing the art of pleasing the great majority.' Yet in *William Tell* that is exactly what his spare, supple style manages to achieve.

The play tells the story of the Swiss rebellion. At a secret council on the Rutli, it is decided that force is the only way out, and that the Austrian fortresses will be stormed at Christmas. Significantly, William Tell has refused to take part in these plans, but is arrested with his son at Altdorf for failing to salute the symbol of Austrian domination. Rudenz, who will become the people's leader, intercedes for Tell with the Austrian governor, Gessler. In a typical example of a tyrant's whim, Tell is offered his life if he can shoot an apple from his son's head. Tell achieves this almost impossible feat, but is again arrested when he proudly announces Gessler would have been killed with the second arrow if the first had in any way harmed Tell's son. Tell then escapes from the barge carrying him to Kussnacht, and manages to kill Gessler on the open road. The revolt is successful. On the way home Tell meets a monk who proudly reveals that he has murdered the Emperor himself. Tell rejects him with horror. The people acclaim Tell as a hero, and Rudenz frees all his serfs.

The mainspring of the play's action is Tell's unwillingness to use force in the face of Austria's arbitrary exercise of naked and aggressive tyranny. This makes his final decision to kill Gessler a key moment in his development and a key moment in the development of the play. What is the essential difference between killing Gessler and killing the Emperor? For a modern audience, surrounded as they are by reports of indiscriminate terrorist bombs in Israel, in New York, in London and in Baghdad, the distinction between these two acts may seem an academic splitting of hairs, but for Schiller's audience it remains crucial. Such is Schiller's power as a dramatist, and so well able is he to point up the difference, that even a modern audience can share in what remains a vital debate about the essential distinction between two acts which on the face of it seem depressingly similar.

It is clear that Tell has been goaded beyond endurance. He finally commits himself to an action which he knows in terms

10

of his personal morality is wrong: the killing of another human being. He puts the social good, the advantage to the society to which he belongs, above his personal sense of what is right and wrong, but he does so with an internal struggle that the audience can share, sympathise with and respect. The killing of the Emperor has been done for the thrill and excitement of achieving the almost impossible.

In one sense, Tell's character becomes less sure and certain as the play progresses. At the start he is determined on independence, requiring to be at one with himself and clear about right and wrong. He distrusts talking and thinking, because they get in the way of instinctive action, and so will not take part in the rebels' deliberations. He knows that if his friends ever present him with the clear moral choice of helping them in need or ignoring them, he will do the right thing. His encounter with Gessler teaches him that this inner harmony is not essential before he can actually take some important action. He can shoot the apple on his boy's head while his inner feelings are in a turmoil of doubt about the rightness of his actions. He applies this self knowledge to the shooting of Gessner. While he is far from certain about the rightness of what he is doing, he takes action, even although his inner self is divided about whether he should or should not commit the deed. He puts the social good above the needs of his divided and uncertain self. As a result he remains not a convinced idealist completely sure of his goals, but a dangerously divided and uncertain human being. When he is faced with the Emperor's murderer, he is looking at his own distorted reflection in the mirror of self-knowledge. This is what he himself is in serious danger of becoming. The audience are expected to share the same self-knowledge. They triumph in man's possible achievement and share in the aim of human freedom, but at the same time the play highlights for them the self doubts and divided certainties which the pursuit of these goals involves. Being heroic involves being prepared to carry the burden of self-doubt and uncertainty: what has been called the 'agony of self-conscious existence'. William Tell is a hero not because he dies gloriously, but because he is prepared to carry this burden of self-knowledge, and continue to live. He has also made an important contribution to the setting up of a free society. Bertolt Brecht in *Die Massnahme* demanded that the committed individual must be prepared to damage his inner convictions for the good of society as a whole. It could be argued that Schiller had said it earlier and said it better.

On 9 May 1805, little more than a year after the enormous success of *William Tell* – which has remained securely in the German repertory ever since, perhaps the most quoted and most familiar of all Schiller's plays – Schiller died in his forty-sixth year. Germany has never forgotten him, and his plays still hold the stage there. Elsewhere the world keeps rediscovering him. He was one of the first grand Romantics, so it was perhaps fitting that in his own day Romantic writers repudiated him for his so-called retreat from what Romanticism stood for. But his plays, his writings and his poetry survive to confound lesser critics.

'Si monumentum requiris circumspice' ('If you need a monument look around you'), they wrote on Sir Christopher Wren's tomb in St Paul's Cathedral. Schiller too has his monument. It exists on paper, and in the minds and hearts of living audiences as his ideas and his incandescent language still set the stage alight.

JOAN OF ARC
(DIE JUNGFRAU VON ORLEANS)

A ROMANTIC TRAGEDY

For James Hogan

CHARACTERS

CHARLES VII
King of France

QUEEN ISABEAU
his mother

AGNÈS SOREL
his mistress

PHILIP THE GOOD
Duke of Burgundy

COUNT DUNOIS
the Bastard

LA HIRE and DU CHATEL
royal officers

ARCHBISHOP OF RHEIMS

CHATILLON
a Burgundian knight

RAOUL
a knight of Lorraine

TALBOT
the English general

LIONEL and FASTOLF
English commanders

MONTGOMERY
a Welshman

COUNCILLORS
from Orléans

AN ENGLISH HERALD

THIBAUT D'ARC
a rich sheep-farmer

MARGOT, LOUISON, and JOAN
his daughters

ETIENNE, CLAUDE-MARIE and RAIMOND
their suitors

BERTRAND
another farmer

APPARITION OF A BLACK KNIGHT

CHARCOAL BURNER
CHARCOAL BURNER'S WIFE
CHARCOAL BURNER'S SON

Soldiers and people, royal servants, bishops, monks, marshals, magistrates, court personnel and other non-speaking characters in the coronation procession.

This translation of *Joan of Arc* was written for the Citizens'
Company and first performed by them at the Citizens' Theatre,
Glasgow, on 9 October 1987, with the following cast:

CHARLES VII, Laurance Rudic

QUEEN ISABEAU, Julia Blalock

AGNÈS SOREL, Ann Lambton

BURGUNDY, Peter Raffan

DUNOIS, Mark Lewis

LA HIRE, Derwent Watson

DU CHATEL, Calum MacAninch

ARCHBISHOP, Brown Derby

THIBAUT / TALBOT, Patrick Hannaway

RAIMOND / LIONEL, Ian Reddington

ETIENNE / MONTGOMERY, Aaron Harris

CLAUDE-MARIE / FASTOLF, Robin Sneller

BERTRAND / SOLDIER IN THE TOWER, Daniel Kash

COUNCILLOR FROM ORLÉANS, Christopher Gee

PAGE TO ISABEAU, Alan McCulloch

MARGOT, Eleanor Slaven

LOUISON, Patti Clark

JOAN, Charon Bourke

WHITE KNIGHT (RAOUL), Robin Sneller

BLACK KNIGHT, Daniel Kash

CHARCOAL BURNER / his WIFE / his SON,
  Harry Gibson

Coronation commentary spoken by Tom Fleming

Director, Robert David MacDonald

Designer, Stewart Laing

Lighting design, Durham Marenghi

Assistant Director, Dafydd Burne-Jones

PROLOGUE

A country landscape. A saint's image in a shrine, and a tall oak tree. THIBAUT D'ARC. His three DAUGHTERS. Three young SHEPHERDS, their suitors.

THIBAUT: Neighbours, and friends: yes, we are Frenchmen still,
　　free citizens and masters of the lands
　　our fathers ploughed before us, for today.
　　Who knows what masters we shall have tomorrow?
　　On every side the English banners float
　　victorious: their cavalry treads down
　　our crops: the gates of Paris have already
　　been opened to the conqueror, and the ancient
　　crown of St Denis has been placed upon
　　the head of a princeling of a foreign line.
　　The rightful heir of France must wander now,
　　an outcast refugee, through his own kingdom.
　　Meanwhile his cousin and the premier peer
　　of France, the Duke of Burgundy, has joined
　　the enemy, led by that bird of prey, his mother.
　　Villages and towns burn all around,
　　and all the while the smoke of ruin rolls
　　nearer and nearer to our peaceful valley.
　　Therefore, dear friends, with God's help, I'm resolved,
　　while I still can, to see my daughters married.
　　In times like these, women need our protection,
　　and true love helps to make our burdens lighter.
　　(*To the first SHEPHERD.*)
　　Etienne, now, you've spoken for my Margot,
　　our fields adjoin: now let your hearts be joined –
　　a good foundation for a happy marriage.
　　Claude-Marie, you say nothing, and Louise
　　looks at the ground? Should I forbid the love
　　of two hearts that have found each other, simply
　　because you have no wealth to offer me?
　　Who *has* wealth nowadays, when farms and houses
　　lie at the mercy of the nearest foe – or fire?

The only stormproof shelter in these times
is a good man's love.

LOUISON: Father!

THIBAUT: Louison!

LOUISON: (*Embracing JOAN.*)   Sister!

THIBAUT: I give you thirty acres each, along
with outbuildings and livestock, and may God
be good to you, as He has been to me.

MARGOT: (*Embracing JOAN.*)
Make Father happy. Follow our example,
and crown his happiness with a triple wedding.

THIBAUT: Go and get ready; the wedding is tomorrow,
and the whole village must be here to celebrate.
(*The two couples go off arm-in-arm.*)
There are your sisters to be married, Joan.
To see them happy is a comfort to my age,
but you, my youngest, cause me pain and grief.

RAIMOND: What are you thinking? Scolding her like that?

THIBAUT: Here is this excellent boy; not one in all
the village is to be compared with him.
For three years now his feelings have been plain,
no less sincere for being unexpressed.
But you rejected him, reserved and cold,
and no one else can win a smile from you.
I see you in the first full flush of youth:
this is your spring, this is your time of Hope,
your beauty is in flower, and still I wait
in vain for Love to flower and come to fruit.
I don't like it at all: it points to some
serious error in Nature when the heart
closes itself to feeling at your age.

RAIMOND: That is enough now, let the girl alone.
Joan's love is like a delicate, tender fruit:
perfection must have time to grow to ripeness.
She still prefers to wander on the hillsides,
and leaves the open heath reluctantly
to come among people and their petty cares.
Sometimes, when I am in the valley, I

watch her, in silent wonder, on the uplands,
standing above her flock, so noble in
appearance, her gaze intently fixed upon
the little world below her, and she seems
to be in touch with higher things, almost
as if she came from some age not our own.

THIBAUT: That is precisely what I do not like!
She avoids the happy company of her sisters,
leaving her bed before first light to seek
the lonely hills: and in those hours of darkness
when folk are gladdest of each other's company,
she slips out, like some solitary owl,
into the dusk and gloom of the haunted night,
making her way up to the crossroads, where
she holds some secret conversation with the winds.
Why does she always choose *that* spot? why is
it there and only there she drives her flocks?
I've watched her sit and think for hours on end,
under the Druid's tree, which Christian souls
will not go near – the place is eerie, some
spirit of evil has lived beneath that tree
since heathen times – the old ones in the village
tell terrifying tales about the tree:
how you can often catch the sound of voices,
strange and uncanny, coming from its dark branches:
once I was passing it myself, at nightfall,
and saw this ghostly woman sitting there,
stretching a withered hand out of her cloak,
as if to say 'Come here!': you may be sure
I quickened my step and offered up a prayer.

RAIMOND: (*Pointing to the image in the shrine.*)
It is the holy influence of the shrine
that brings your daughter here, and not the Devil.

THIBAUT: Oh, no! No! Not for nothing have I had
warnings in dreams and visions. Three times now
I've seen her, sitting on the royal throne
in Rheims Cathedral, on her head a crown
of seven stars, and in her hand a sceptre,

out of which three golden lilies sprouted,
while I, her father, and her sisters, and
princes, bishops, lords, the King himself
all knelt to her – how does such splendour come
to our poor house? It presages disaster.
The dream was sent to show me, and to warn me
about the idle vanity of her heart.
She is ashamed because she is low-born:
just because God has blessed her, outwardly
and inwardly, with faculties beyond
the other shepherd girls here in the valley,
she is puffed up with spiritual pride.
By that sin fell the angels: pride it is
gives Satan purchase on the souls of men.

RAIMOND: Who is more modest, or more virtuous than
this child of yours? Has she not made herself
the willing servant of her elder sisters?
Her qualities would raise her far above
all others, yet you see her, like a maid,
performing the most menial tasks in quiet
humility. The livestock and the planting
thrive on her management: whatever she
sets her hand to is rewarded with
amazing, inexplicable good fortune.

THIBAUT: Yes, inexplicable. I feel a sort
of shudder at a blessing of this kind.
Enough – I'll say no more – I do not wish
to say another word. Should I accuse
my own dear child? All I can do is warn her,
and pray for her. Warn her, though, I must,
not to go near the tree, nor be alone,
not dig for roots, nor to prepare concoctions,
nor scratch out secret patterns in the sand.
The spirit world is easily aroused:
it lies in wait, under the thinnest cover,
for the slightest word to call it into life.
Do not be on your own, then: it was in
the wilderness that Satan tempted Christ.

(*Enter BERTRAND, carrying a helmet.*)

RAIMOND: Quiet! Bertrand, back from town. Look what
 he's carrying.

BERTRAND: You look surprised to see
 me with this strange contraption.

THIBAUT: Yes, we are.
 How did you come by it, and why should you
 bring this ill-omen to a land of peace?
 (*JOAN, who up to now has taken no interest in the scene,*
 gradually becomes attentive, and moves nearer in.)

BERTRAND: I hardly know myself how I came by it.
 I was buying iron tools in Vaucouleurs:
 there was a crowd of people in the market –
 some refugees had brought bad news from Orléans –
 the whole town seemed to have gathered in alarm,
 and as I forced a passage through the crowd,
 a dark-faced gypsy woman, carrying
 this helmet, came right up to me, and stared
 at me, and said 'My son, you're looking for a helmet
 I know you're looking for one. There! Take this!
 It's yours for next to nothing.' And I said:
 'Go to the soldiers; I don't need a helmet,
 I'm just a farmer.' But she wouldn't be
 content with that, and went on 'Who can dare
 to say he does or doesn't need a helmet?
 A steel roof for the head is nowadays
 better than a stone one for the house.'
 She kept on, following me through the streets,
 forcing the thing on me I didn't want.
 I looked at it, saw it was fine and bright,
 and fit to go on any great knight's head,
 and as I weighed it doubtfully in my hand
 wondering at the strangeness of it all,
 the woman suddenly was gone, the stream
 of people carried her away, and left
 me standing with the helmet in my hands.

JOAN: (*Grasping for it eagerly.*)
 Give it to me!

BERTRAND: What would *you* want with it?
    It's nothing for a girl.

JOAN: (*Snatching the helmet from him.*)
                        The helmet's mine!

THIBAUT: What is the matter with the girl?

RAIMOND: Just let
    her have it. It will suit her well: she has
    a man's heart in that body. Only think
    how she fought off that wolf that caused such havoc
    among our flocks, the terror of our shepherds;
    how, on her own, the lion-hearted girl
    fought with the beast and tore the lamb away
    out of its very jaws. However brave
    the one who wears this helmet, it could never
    suit any more than her.

THIBAUT: (*To BERTRAND.*) But tell us what
    the news was which the refugees had brought.

BERTRAND: Pray Heaven help the King and spare the country!
    We have been beaten in two heavy battles.
    The enemy is in possession of
    the whole of France up to the Loire, and now
    he brings his whole force to besiege Orléans.

THIBAUT: Heaven protect the King!

BERTRAND: Artillery
    is being brought in from all sides in countless
    quantities, and like a swarm of bees
    darkening the hive in summer, or a cloud
    of locusts falling from the darkened sky
    and covering the fields for miles around,
    a swarm of soldiers poured into the plains
    around Orléans: and in the camp is heard
    a Babel of tongues, confused and deafening:
    since the powerful Duke of Burgundy has brought
    his vassals here as well, from Luxemburg
    Liege and Hennegau, Namur, Brabant,
    Ghent, Zeeland, Utrecht, Holland, and as far
    North as West Friesland, to besiege Orléans.

THIBAUT: That is the saddest thing about this struggle,

that French arms should be used against France herself.

BERTRAND: And one can see the old queen-mother too,
    the arrogant Isabella of Bavaria,
    riding in full armour through the camp,
    stirring the men up, with her poisonous speeches
    against the King, her son.

THIBAUT: God's curse on her! And may He bring her down
    as He did Jezebel.

BERTRAND: The siege is being led by the destroyer
    of the Moors, the powerful Salisbury,
    along with Lionel, a lion indeed,
    and Talbot, who mows down our men in battle.
    They have all sworn, in their overweening pride,
    to give our women to their soldiers, and
    to put our soldiers to the sword.
    They have put up four observation towers
    to overlook the town: and from above
    the Earl of Salisbury looks down and counts
    the people hurrying about the streets.
    Thousands of tons of missiles have been hurled
    into the town: the churches lie in ruins,
    and the great tower of Notre-Dame hangs down
    its noble head. And they have undermined
    the walls with powder magazines, so that the town
    stands terror-stricken on a pit of Hell,
    expecting every hour to fly in pieces.

(*JOAN listens with intense attention, putting on the helmet.*)

THIBAUT: Where were the swords of our brave leaders, then?
    Saintrailles, La Hire, Dunois the Bastard, that
    the enemy was able to push forward
    so irresistibly? Where was the King?
    Was he content to watch his country's ruin,
    to see his cities all reduced to rubble?

BERTRAND: The court is at Chinon, but he lacks troops,
    he cannot stay in the field: and what use is
    the leader's courage or the hero's arms,
    when panic paralyses all the army?
    A terror, almost as if ordained by Heaven,

has seized upon the hearts even of the bravest.
The generals issue their commands in vain:
like sheep that huddle fearfully together
at the howling of the wolf, all Frenchmen now,
regardless of their former reputation
for valour, seek the safety of their castles.
One knight alone, or so I hear, has raised
a little band of soldiers for the King.

JOAN: (*Quickly.*) What is his name?

BERTRAND: Baudricour. But he
will have no little difficulty outwitting
the enemy's intelligence, if he has
two English armies following at his heels.

JOAN: Where has he halted? Tell me, if you know.

BERTRAND: Not more than one day's march from Vaucouleurs.

THIBAUT: What's it to you, girl? Asking about things
that don't concern you.

BERTRAND: They in Vaucouleurs,
seeing the enemy so powerful, and no hope
of any more protection from the King,
have all resolved to go over to Burgundy.
That way we shall escape a foreign yoke,
staying with our own royal line: who knows
but that we may not serve the King again,
if he and Burgundy are reconciled.

JOAN: (*As if inspired.*) No treaties! No surrender! The deliverer
is on the way, already armed for battle.
Before Orléans the enemy's luck will founder:
his cup is full, now it is harvest time.
The virgin with the sickle in her hand
will mow him down in his pride, and snatch his glory
back down from the stars where he had lodged it.
No weakening! No retreat! Before the crops
have turned to gold, before the moon is full,
no English horse shall water at the Loire.

BERTRAND: Oh, come, the age of miracles is over.

JOAN: No! It is not! A white dove will fly up,
brave as an eagle, to attack these vultures

that tear our land apart. She will bring down
the traitor Burgundy, Talbot, the hundred-handed,
the heaven-stormer, and that Salisbury,
profaner of the temple, and all those
swaggering islanders shall be driven before her
like lambs to slaughter: God will be at her side,
the God of battles, who will seek her out,
a trembling virgin, through whom he will show
his power on earth, for he is King of Kings.
THIBAUT: What has possessed the girl?
RAIMOND: It is the helmet
gives her these warlike thoughts. Look at your daughter!
Her eyes are flashing and her cheeks are flushed.
JOAN: And shall this country fall? this country of
such fame, more beautiful than any that
the sun shines on; this paradise of lands,
which God loves as the apple of his eye:
is it to submit to foreign shackles?
In France the heathen power was forced to halt;
the ashes of St Louis rest in France;
from France they left to free the Holy Land.
BERTRAND: (*Astonished.*) Listen to her! Where does she receive
this revelation from? You, her father:
God has given you a marvellous child.
JOAN: We shall not have our own kings any more:
the King, whose line means he can never die,
shall vanish from the earth, the King whose arm
protects the sacred plough, shields the pasture lands
makes the earth fertile, leads his subjects out
to Freedom, gathers his cities round his throne,
frightens the wicked and protects the weak,
who feels no envy, since he is the greatest,
who is both man and angel of compassion
upon this hostile earth. The throne which shines
with gold is a sure refuge for the outcast.
There, there is power and mercy to be found,
to confound the guilty, while the just draw near
in trust, to sport with lions at its feet.

How can the stranger king, come from abroad,
none of whose ancestors have found repose
within this land, how then can he love it?
He has not shared his youth with our young men,
our language sparks no feelings in his heart,
how can he be a father to his children?

THIBAUT: Now God protect the country and the king!
We are just peaceful countrymen, who have
no notion how to wield a sword, or curb
a war-horse: let us wait in patience,
to see whom victory will make our master.
God will decide the fortunes of this war:
our master is the one who is anointed
and crowned at Rheims. Come on now, back to work!
and mind our business. We can let the great
and powerful of the earth decide its fate.
Indifferent to destruction at the hand
of war, the earth remains: ours is the land.
Let flames devour our villages, and let
the warhorse trample down the ripening grain:
with a new spring new seed is born again:
houses can be rebuilt: men can forget.
(*All go out except JOAN.*)

JOAN: Mountains, much-loved meadows, dear, quiet valleys,
Joan bids you all a long, a last farewell.
The fields I watered, and the trees I planted,
show fresh and green again. Farewell! the caves
the cool springs, and the valley's voice, the echo
that would send back the songs I sang before;
farewell, you shall not see Joan any more.

Scenes of the joys of all my quiet days,
I leave you now behind, beyond, beneath.
Scatter yourselves, my lambs, and take your ways
to wander shepherdless upon your heath:
for I have now another flock to graze,
upon the field of danger, blood and death.
The spirit calls to me with tongues of fire,
what drives me is not earthly, vain desire.

He who in Sinai, on the mountain height,
appeared to Moses in the bush of flame,
and ordered him to stand in Pharaoh's sight:
He who to the shepherd David came,
and chose the boy His champion in the fight,
who always favoured shepherds in His name;
He spoke out of the branches of the tree:
'Go forth! Bear witness in this world for Me.

With raw, rough iron your body shall be girt,
your woman's breast shall be encased in steel;
the love of Man may never move your heart,
Earth's sinful pleasures you shall never feel;
no marriage of which you shall be a part,
no child your woman's mission to fulfil.
But with war's honours I shall raise your name
above all women, to undying fame.

For when the last defeat of France seems near,
when in the battle even the bravest fail,
then will My standard become yours to bear,
and, like an eager thresher, with your flail
bring down the haughty conqueror in fear,
reverse his fortunes, over him prevail.
To France's hero-sons salvation bring,
free Rheims, and crown your true and lawful King!'

Heaven has vouchsafed to me a sign:
this helmet He has sent, it comes from Him.
His power in the metal is divine.
I flame with the courage of the Cherubim,
driving me on towards the battle line.
There, in the storm of steel, I sink, I swim:
I hear the war-cry, turn to face the foe:
the charger rears, and all the trumpets blow!

End of Prologue.

ACT ONE

The court of King CHARLES at Chinon.

DUNOIS: I cannot tolerate this any more.
    I must renounce this King, who has forgotten
    himself so shamefully. My heart bleeds in
    my breast, and I could weep hot tears to see
    our royal France quartered by the swords of thieves,
    the noble cities, grown old with the kingdom,
    giving their rusty keys up to the enemy,
    while we waste valuable time here doing nothing.
    I hear Orléans is besieged, fly
    from furthest Normandy, thinking to find
    the king in arms and at his army's head:
    instead I find him here, surrounded by
    mountebanks, and minstrels, solving riddles,
    and giving gallant parties for his mistress,
    as if the land was wallowing in peace!
    The Constable has left him, could not stand
    the situation any longer: and
    I too am resolved to abandon him,
    and leave him to his wretched fate.
DU CHATEL: Here comes the King now!
CHARLES: The Constable has sent me back his sword,
    and given notice that he will not serve
    me any longer. In which case – dear God! –
    all we are rid of is a troublesome man,
    who sought to rule us quite without condition.
DUNOIS: In such a time I would not be disposed
    to greet the loss of *any* man so lightly.
CHARLES: You say that just from love of contradiction:
    you were no friend of his while he was here.
DUNOIS: He was an arrogant, offensive fool
    who never knew when to stop – but for this once,
    he knows. He knows the time to leave a cause
    is when there's no more honour to be gained.
CHARLES: We're in one of our pleasant moods, I see:

I shan't disturb you. Du Chatel! there are
ambassadors from old King René, famous
singers; they must be entertained, and well.
See there's a golden chain for each of them.
And what is so amusing, pray?
DUNOIS: To hear
how chains of gold fall from your lips like spittle.
DU CHATEL: Your Majesty! There is no money left
in the treasury.
CHARLES: Then find some. Famous artists
shall never leave my court without reward.
It's they who make our sterile sceptre flower,
who weave the green, unfading leaves of life
into the barren circle of the crown.
Their mastery places them upon a level
with their masters: they set up the thrones
of their frail harmless kingdoms on their wish
alone, and are not circumscribed by space.
This higher world thus equally belongs
to those who rule men, and those who make their songs.
DU CHATEL: Your Majesty! as long as there were still
expedients, I tried to keep things from you:
now finally, necessity bids me speak.
You have no more to give away, – good grief! –
you have no more to live on from tomorrow!
The high tide of your fortune has retreated;
your treasury is at its lowest ebb.
The troops have not been paid yet, and are grumbling,
threatening to withdraw. I hardly know
what to advise to keep your royal household
provided with the bare necessities,
let alone in any fitting state.
CHARLES: Mortgage the royal customs duties, and
get the Lombards to advance some money.
DU CHATEL: Sire! the customs duties are already
mortgaged for three years in advance.
DUNOIS: Meanwhile
both lands and pledges go to rack and ruin.

33

CHARLES: We still have several rich and fertile provinces.
DUNOIS: As long as God and Talbot's armies spare them.
    If Orléans is taken, you can go
    and be a shepherd, like your friend King René.
CHARLES: You never can resist a jibe at his
    expense, but it was this king, who, although
    dispossessed of all his lands, sent me
    those rich gifts, even today.
DUNOIS: Heaven forfend,
    I hope he did not send the crown of Naples!
    I hear it's going cheap, since he has taken
    to playing shepherd.
CHARLES: That is just a game,
    a sort of joke he plays upon himself,
    to make an innocent world of make-believe,
    in a rough age of harsh realities.
    But what he wishes, which is truly great,
    is to reintroduce the good old times
    when courtly love stirred men to deeds of courage,
    and noble women sat in arbitration
    on each nice point of etiquette. This is
    the age in which the old man still lives happily,
    seeking to recreate it here, like some
    celestial city in the clouds, the way it is
    described in the old songs. For this he has
    set up a court of love, to which brave knights
    can make their pilgrimage, where women are
    enthroned in majesty and chastity,
    where pure love once again can be the rule:
    and he has picked me out as Prince of Love.
DUNOIS: I am not yet so far degenerate
    as to despise the paramount sway of Love,
    seeing it is to him I owe my name,
    my birth and everything that I inherit.
    My father was the Prince of Orléans,
    who never met the heart he could not win,
    nor the enemy that could stand against him.
    If you wish to deserve the title 'Prince

of Love', then be the bravest of the brave.
My reading in those old books tells me that
love was always paired with chivalry,
and it was heroes sat at the round table,
not shepherds, if I am not misinformed.
The man who does not fight to defend Beauty
does not deserve to be rewarded by her.
This is the battlefield! Fight for your father's crown!
With your sword defend your property,
and the honour of all those noble ladies. Once
you have, through streams of enemy blood,
won back the crown of your ancestors, well, then
will be the time and suitable occasion
to crown yourself with myrtle.

CHARLES: (*To a COURTIER who enters.*) Yes, what is it?

COURTIER: Councillors from Orléans begging audience.

CHARLES: Show them in.
    (*Exit COURTIER.*)   They will implore my help.
What can I do, who cannot help myself?
    (*Enter three COUNCILLORS.*)
Welcome, my loyal citizens of Orléans!
How are things with the city? Is she still
keeping the enemy off with her usual courage?

COUNCILLOR: Alas, Your Majesty, the city is
in the direst straits, and every hour
the situation grows more desperate.
The outer walls are breached, the enemy
gains ground with each assault; the battlements
are undefended, for the men are all
thrown unremittingly against the enemy,
and few enough of them return. Meanwhile
the plague of hunger menaces the city.
Therefore Count Rochepierre, the town commander,
has, in this terrible emergency,
according to the rights of war, agreed
with the besiegers, to give up the city
on the twelfth day, if, within that time,

35

no force, sufficient to relieve the siege,
has signalled its appearance in the field.
(*DUNOIS makes a violent movement of anger.*)

CHARLES: So little time.

COUNCILLOR: And so we come to you,
on a safe-conduct from the enemy,
to implore Your Majesty to pity us,
and send us help within the time allotted,
or else the city must surrender.

DUNOIS: Could
Saintrailles have given his sanction to so vile
a treaty?

COUNCILLOR: No, my lord. As long as he
was living, there would never have been talk
of peace or of surrender.

DUNOIS: So he is dead?

COUNCILLOR: He fell heroically on the city walls,
fighting for his King.

CHARLES: Saintrailles is dead!
In that one man I lose an army.
(*A KNIGHT enters and speaks a few words in a low voice to
DUNOIS, who exclaims in surprise.*)

DUNOIS: That as well!

CHARLES: What now?

DUNOIS: The Earl of Douglas sends to say
the Scottish troops have mutinied, and threaten
to withdraw if their arrears of pay are not
discharged immediately.

CHARLES: Du Chatel!

DU CHATEL: (*Shrugging.*)
I cannot help Your Majesty.

CHARLES: Pawn, promise,
all that we have, even to half our kingdom…

DU CHATEL: It will not help – there have already been
too many promises.

CHARLES: The Scottish soldiers are the best I have!
They cannot leave me now, not now, they cannot!

COUNCILLOR: (*Falling on his knees.*)
    Help us, Your Majesty! Think of our need!
CHARLES: (*Despairingly.*)
        Can I stamp armies from the ground? Will corn
        grow in the palm of my hand? Tear me in pieces,
        rip out my heart and turn it into coin.
        Blood I can give you, but not men nor money.
        (*He sees SOREL coming in, and hurries to her with arms
        outstretched.*)
        Agnès! My love, my life! You come in time
        to save me from despair. While I can still
        fly to your arms, all is not lost, since you
        are mine still.
SOREL: (*Entering carrying a casket.*)
                        Oh, my dear Lord!
        (*She looks round anxiously.*)   Du Chatel? Dunois?
        Is this true, then?
DU CHATEL: I fear so.
SOREL: Is the need
        really so urgent? Will the troops withdraw
        for want of pay?
DU CHATEL: I am afraid so.
SOREL: (*Pressing the casket on him.*) Here!
        Here is gold! Here are my jewels! Melt
        my silver down! Sell, mortgage all my castles!
        Arrange a loan on my Provence estates!
        Turn everything to money, see the armies
        are satisfied. Go now and lose no time.
        (*Pushing him out.*)
CHARLES: Well, Dunois? Du Chatel? Am I still poor,
        while I possess this jewel among women?
        Nobly born as I am – even the blood
        of Valois is no better – she would be
        an ornament to any throne in the world.
        But she despises them, and wishes only
        to be my love, and to be seen to be it.
        Has she ever accepted from my hand
        a present more expensive than a flower

in wintertime, or some exotic fruit?
She will accept no sacrifice from me,
and yet she sacrifices all for me,
wagering all her property and fortune
to prop the fortunes of my tottering house.

DUNOIS: She is as mad as you are, throwing all
she has into a burning house, and trying
to put the fire out with a leaky bucket.
She will not save you, she will merely bring
herself to ruin with you –

SOREL: Don't believe him!
He has risked his life a dozen times for you,
and now he's angry because I risk my money.
Have I not already given you
and freely, all I have of much more value
than gold or jewels, and am I now supposed
to keep my wretched fortune to myself?
Let us get rid of all superfluous
luxuries, let me set you an example
of renunciation. Turn your courtiers
into an army, turn your gold into steel,
decide now to throw everything you have
away, to win your crown back. Come with me!
Come! We shall share all dangers and privations;
we'll ride together, we'll expose our bodies
to the burning arrows of the sun; the clouds
will be our canopy, and the stones our pillows.
The roughest soldier will stop grumbling, when
he sees his King, no better than the meanest,
enduring and surmounting want and toil.

CHARLES: (*Smiling.*) A prophecy begins to be fulfilled,
a nun at Clermont made to me; she said
a woman would make me victor over all
my enemies, and win back my fathers' crown.
I looked for her among the enemy camp,
thinking to make peace with my mother. But
here is the heroine who will lead me on
to Rheims, and in whose love I shall find victory!

SOREL: You will find it in the swords of your brave friends.

CHARLES: I have great hopes of discord in their camp;
    I have intelligence that all is not
    just as it was between the Lords of England,
    and cousin Burgundy. I therefore sent
    La Hire to take a message to the Duke,
    to see if we can bring our furious kinsman
    back to the path of loyalty and duty.
    I expect him back at any moment.

DU CHATEL: (*At the window.*)   He
    has just dismounted in the courtyard.

CHARLES: Now,
    this welcome messenger will let us know
    whether it's victory or retreat. La Hire!
    (*Going to meet LA HIRE as he enters.*)
    Do you bring us hope or not? Be brief.
    What are we to expect?

LA HIRE: Nothing, but what
    your sword can get from him.

CHARLES: So he will not
    be reconciled. How did he take my message?

LA HIRE: First, and before he even gives an ear
    to your proposals, he demands that you
    deliver Du Chatel to him, the man he calls
    his father's murderer.

CHARLES: And what if we
    refuse this unacceptable condition?

LA HIRE: The treaty may be looked on as still-born.

CHARLES: And did you, as I asked you, challenge him
    to fight with me in single combat, at
    the bridge at Montereau, where his father died?

LA HIRE: I threw your gauntlet down, and let him know
    you would lay by your dignity, and fight
    for your kingdom as a simple knight. He answered
    that he could see no need to fight for what
    he had already, but that if you were
    so eager for a fight, then you would find him

at Orléans, where he means to go tomorrow:
and then he laughed, and turned his back on me.
CHARLES: And was there no voice raised in Parliament
on the side of justice?
LA HIRE: No. That voice was drowned
in party rage. Parliament has decreed,
you and your house have forfeited the crown.
DUNOIS: The arrogance of slaves who would be masters!
CHARLES: Did you make no approaches to my mother?
LA HIRE: Your mother!
CHARLES: Yes. How did she view the business?
LA HIRE: (*After a moment of consideration.*)
When I arrived at St Denis, it was
the day of the coronation, and all Paris
was decked out, as if for a victory.
In every street there were triumphal arches,
through which the King of England passed in state.
The road was strewn with flowers, and the mob
crowded around the carriage, yelling and shouting,
as if France had just won her finest victory.
SOREL: Shouting and yelling as they tread upon
the heart of their own true and loving king.
LA HIRE: I saw the boy, young Harry of Lancaster,
on the throne of St Louis, with both his proud uncles,
Bedford and Gloucester, standing at his side,
while the Duke of Burgundy went on his knees
before the throne to swear his land's allegiance.
CHARLES: Oh my unworthy cousin! False, disloyal!
LA HIRE: The boy was scared, and stumbled as he climbed
the steps up to the throne. The people muttered
something about ill omens, and a laugh
rang out among the crowd, and, at that moment
your mother, the old queen, stepped forward, and...
I am appalled to speak of it...
CHARLES: What happened?
LA HIRE: She picked the boy up in her arms, and set him
up on your fathers' throne.
CHARLES: Oh, mother, mother!

LA HIRE: Even the Burgundian troops, inured
  by now to blood and fury, blushed to see it.
  She guessed what they were thinking, and she turned
  to face the crowd, and raised her voice to say:
  'Frenchmen, you have me to thank for this.
  I have cut down the old, sick trunk and planted
  the healthy sapling, and have saved you from
  the misbegotten son of an idiot father.'
  (*The KING covers his face. SOREL runs to him and folds him
  in her arms. All present express their disgust and horror.*)
DUNOIS: Wolf bitch! Bloodthirsty, rabid monster!
CHARLES: (*After a pause, to the COUNCILLORS.*)
  Well, you have heard how matters stand with us.
  Go back to Orléans, waste no more time here,
  and tell my loyal city: I release her
  from any oath of fealty sworn to me.
  Let her seek mercy from the Duke of Burgundy.
DUNOIS: What is this, Sire? Will you give up Orléans?
COUNCILLOR: My royal master! Do not take away
  your hand from us. Oh, do not give your loyal
  city up to the tyranny of England!
  She is the brightest jewel in your crown,
  and none has been more faithful to your fathers.
DUNOIS: Have we been beaten, then? Is it allowed
  to quit the field before one blow is struck
  to save the city? Is that how you think
  to give away, with one lightly spoken word,
  the finest city from the heart of France?
CHARLES: Enough blood has been shed, and pointlessly!
  The heavy hand of Heaven is against me.
  My armies are defeated in every battle:
  my parliament disowns me: in my capital
  my people greet my enemy with frenzy:
  my next of kin abandon and betray me:
  and even my own mother suckles the brood
  of hostile foreigners at the breast. Therefore
  we shall draw back to the South bank of the Loire,

and submit ourselves to the all-powerful hand
of Heaven, which fights upon the English side.
SOREL: Heaven forfend that we, despairing of
our cause, should turn our backs upon our country.
Your brave heart just cannot have framed those words.
My King's heroic spirit has been broken
by the vile acts of his unnatural mother.
You will soon be yourself again, and able
to counter bravely all the blows that Fate
is dealing you.
CHARLES: (*Gloomily.*) But might it not be true?
A dark and terrible curse is on the house
of Valois. God has cast us out. My mother's
depravity has brought the Furies down
upon our house. For twenty years my father
was mad, three elder brothers died before me.
It is the will of Heaven that the house
of Valois perishes with Charles the Sixth.
SOREL: It will rise again in you! Have confidence
in yourself. Oh, it is not in vain that Heaven
was kinder to you than to all your brothers,
placing you, although the youngest son,
upon a throne you never could have looked for.
Your gentle nature is the medicine
for all the wounds that party rage inflicts
on France. You will put out the angry fires
of civil war – my heart tells me you will –
restore peace and our ancient monarchy.
CHARLES: Not I. These rough and storm-tossed times demand
a stronger steersman at the helm. I might
have made a peaceful nation happy, but
not this desperate and savage people.
I cannot force my way through with my sword
into those hearts that hate has closed against me.
SOREL: The people are dazzled, stunned: a sort of madness
possesses them, but that will pass. The day
is not far off when their old love for their
ancestral king, the love that's planted deep

42

in every Frenchman's heart, will reawaken,
and jealousy along with it, and the ancient
aversion that exists between two nations.
The victor will be destroyed by his own good fortune,
That is why you must not be too hasty
to quit the field, but fight for every inch
of ground, defend Orléans, as if your life
depended on it. Rather let all the ferries
be sunk and all the bridges burnt that carry you
over your kingdom's border, across the Loire
as if across the Styx.

CHARLES: What I could do
I have already done, I offered myself
in single combat for the crown. I was refused.
My people's blood is being spilt in vain:
my cities are collapsing into dust.
Should I be like the unnatural mother, who
let her own child be cut in two? Oh, no!
I shall renounce my child, so it may live.

DUNOIS: What, Sire? Is that the language of a king?
Is that the way one gives away a crown?
The meanest of your subjects stakes his life
and all he has on what he loves and hates.
Let once the bloody sign of civil war
be hung out, and all men are partisans.
The ploughman leaves the plough, the housewife leaves
her distaff, children and old men take arms,
the townsfolk fire their cities, and the peasant
sets fire to his crops, to do you harm
or good, whichever will express his will.
He gives no quarter, and expects none, when
he fights for his honour, for his gods, or idols.
Stop this show of self-pity, then, which ill
becomes a king, and let war take its course
and burn its fury out. It was not you
who set it recklessly alight. The people
must sacrifice itself for King and Country.
That is the law and fate of nations, and

there is no Frenchman who would have it otherwise.
The nation is not worthy of the name,
that will not risk its all to save its honour.
CHARLES: (*To the COUNCILLORS.*)
    Expect no more from me, I can do nothing.
    God protect you.
DUNOIS: May the god of battles
    from now on turn his back on you, as you
    have turned your back on your ancestral kingdom.
    I shall desert you, since you desert yourself.
    Not all the might of Burgundy and England,
    but your own cowardice costs you your throne.
    The kings of France were heroes once, but you
    have had unsoldierly breeding, it would seem.
    (*To the COUNCILLORS.*)
    The King has given you up, but I shall throw
    myself into the fight for Orléans,
    my native city, and perish in its ruins.
    (*He starts to leave SOREL detains him.*)
SOREL: No! Do not let him leave you in this anger.
    His words are harsh, but his heart is true as gold.
    This is the man who loves you, who has shed
    his blood for you before. Dunois, confess,
    the heat of the moment made you go too far.
    And you, forgive him what was said in haste.
    Oh, come, the pair of you. Let me reconcile
    your hearts, before this disagreement bursts
    into unquenchable destructive flame.
    (*DUNOIS stares fixedly at the KING, waiting for an answer.*)
CHARLES: (*To DU CHATEL.*)
    We cross the Loire. See my equipment packed.
DUNOIS: (*Quickly, to SOREL.*) Goodbye.
    (*He turns quickly and goes out, the COUNCILLORS following him.*)
SOREL: Oh, if he leaves us, we are truly lost.
    La Hire, go after him – try to bring him round.
    (*LA HIRE goes out.*)

CHARLES: Well, is the crown the only thing in the world?
Is it such pain and grief to part with it?
I'll tell you something that is harder still
to bear, and that is being imposed upon
by obstinate and domineering bullies,
being dependent on the favour of
a lot of arrogant, self-opinionated
vassals. That is the really hard thing for
a noble heart to bear, and bitterer far
than yielding to one's fate.
(*To DU CHATEL.*)   Obey your orders!

DU CHATEL: (*Throwing himself at the KING's feet.*)
Your Majesty!

CHARLES: I have decided. Not another word!

DU CHATEL: Conclude peace with the Duke of Burgundy.
There is no other way to save yourself.

CHARLES: Is that what you advise? And is it your blood
that will be used to sign this treaty with?

DU CHATEL: Here is my head. I have risked it often enough
in battle for you. Now I willingly
place it upon the block for you. Appease
the Duke. Deliver me to everything
his rage can do to me, and let my blood
put out the fires of this ancient hatred.

CHARLES: (*Looks at him for a moment, moved and silent.*)
Is it true then? Are things as bad as that?
My friends, who see into my heart, propose
I tread the path of shame to my deliverance?
Yes, now I see how low I must have fallen,
if no one any longer trusts my honour.

DU CHATEL: Just think –

CHARLES: Say nothing! Do not make me angry.
If I had to abandon twenty thrones,
I would not save myself at the expense
of a friend's life. Now do as you were ordered.
See that my necessaries are embarked.

DU CHATEL: At once.
(*He rises and leaves, SOREL bursts into violent sobbing.*)

CHARLES: (*Taking her hand.*)
　　Agnès, do not be sad. Beyond the Loire
　　there is another France, and we are travelling
　　towards a happier land. A milder sky
　　unmarred by any cloud smiles on us there,
　　the winds blow softer, and we are received
　　with gentler customs: it is the land of song,
　　and life and love may flower more freely there.
SOREL: That I should ever have lived to see this day!
　　The King in banishment, the son compelled
　　to leave his fathers' house, to turn his back
　　upon the cradle of his childhood. Oh,
　　my dear, dear country! Now we have to leave you,
　　and we shall never again return in joy.
　　(*LA HIRE returns.*)
　　You are alone. You have not brought him back?
　　(*Looking at him more closely.*)
　　La Hire, what is it? What is that look supposed
　　to mean? Is there some new catastrophe?
LA HIRE: Catastrophe has spent itself: the sun
　　shines out once more.
SOREL: 　　　　　　　　What do you mean?
LA HIRE: (*To the KING.*) 　　　　　　　Call back
　　the councillors from Orléans.
CHARLES: 　　　　　　　Why, what has happened?
LA HIRE: Call them back. Your fortune's tide has turned.
　　A battle has been fought – you are victorious!
SOREL: Victorious! The music of that word!
CHARLES: La Hire! you are deceived with groundless rumours.
　　Victorious! I've no more faith in victories,
LA HIRE: You will soon believe in greater miracles.
　　Here is the Archbishop, bringing the Bastard
　　back to your arms…
SOREL: 　　　　　　The fairest flower of victory
　　is to bring peace and reconciliation.
　　(*Enter the ARCHBISHOP of Rheims, DUNOIS, DU CHATEL
　　and a knight in armour, RAOUL.*)

46

ARCHBISHOP: (*Leading the BASTARD to the KING, and*
joining their hands.) Princes, embrace! Let bitterness and discord
vanish, since Heaven declares itself for us.
(*DUNOIS embraces the KING.*)
CHARLES: Put me out of doubt and of amazement.
What does this solemn seriousness portend?
What has brought about this sudden change?
ARCHBISHOP: (*Bringing the KNIGHT forward to the*
KING.) Speak!
RAOUL: We had brought sixteen companies to the field,
men of Lorraine, to reinforce your armies,
under the leadership of Baudricourt,
from Vaucouleurs. When we had reached the heights
by Vermanton, and gone down to the valley
of the Yonne, there stood the enemy upon
the plain in front of us, and when we looked
behind us, weapons glittered there as well.
We saw ourselves surrounded on all sides.
There was no hope of victory or flight.
The bravest hearts were dashed, and, in despair,
each man began to lay aside his weapons.
And while the generals discussed among
themselves what or what not to do, and still
unable to decide – before our eyes,
a miracle! Suddenly, a girl stepped out
of the depths of the woods, a helmet on her head
like some goddess of war, and beautiful
yet at the same time terrifying. Her hair
fell in dark curls around her neck; a sort
of heavenly aura seemed to play about
her figure, as she raised her voice, to say:
'What are you afraid of, Frenchmen? Up,
attack the enemy: even if he should have
more soldiers than there are sands in the sea,
God and the Blessed Virgin lead you on!'
And then she seized the flag out of the hand
of the standard-bearer, and with dignity
and irresistible audacity,

strode to the head of the column. We, struck dumb
with wonder, almost as if against our wills,
followed the flag and her who carried it,
and made an onslaught on the enemy,
who, utterly amazed, stood motionless,
staring at the miracle taking place
before their very eyes – but suddenly,
as if the fear of God was in them, they
threw their weapons down, and turned and fled.
The entire army scattered across the field:
commands were useless, and the officers rallied
the men in vain: without a backward glance
the panic-stricken men and horses plunged
into the river-bed, and let themselves
be slaughtered without the least show of resistance.
It was no battle – it was butchery!
Two thousand enemy dead lie on the field,
not counting those the river swallowed up:
on our side, not a single man was lost.

CHARLES: My God, that's strange! Miraculous and strange!

SOREL: You say a young girl worked this miracle?
Where is she from? Who is she?

RAOUL: Who she is
she will reveal to no one but the King.
She calls herself a prophetess, sent by Heaven,
and promises to save Orléans before
the moon has changed. The men believe in her;
they're spoiling for a battle. She herself
follows the army and will soon be here.
(*Bells are heard, and the clashing of weapons.*)
You hear that noise? The people welcome her.

CHARLES: (*To DU CHATEL.*)
Have her brought in.
(*To the ARCHBISHOP.*) What should one make of this?
A young girl brings me victory, and at
the very moment only God could help me?
That's hardly in the normal course of Nature:
might one not – Archbishop – trust in miracles?

48

MANY VOICES: (*Offstage.*)

The maid! The maid! Hail the deliverer!

CHARLES: She's here!

(*To DUNOIS.*)   Sit in my place, Dunois, we'll see

just how miraculous this young girl is.

If she is inspired and sent by God,

she will know how to tell which is the King.

(*DUNOIS sits with the KING on his right, and SOREL next to him, the ARCHBISHOP and the rest opposite him, so that the area in the middle of the stage is clear. JOAN enters, accompanied by the COUNCILLORS and a number of KNIGHTS, who fill the rear of the stage; she steps forward, with dignity, and scrutinises the assembly one by one.*)

DUNOIS: (*After a deep and solemn silence.*)

Are you the miracle-worker, then, the girl who all…

JOAN: (*Interrupting him, looking at him clear-eyed and with dignity.*) Bastard of Orléans! Would you tempt your God? Get off that chair; it is no place for you.

My heavenly mission is to one far greater.

(*She walks resolutely up to the KING, goes on one knee before him, getting up again at once. All present express their astonishment. DUNOIS leaves his seat, and a space is left empty in front of the KING.*)

CHARLES: You see my face today for the first time.

Where does this knowledge come from?

JOAN: I saw you,

when no one else saw you, apart from God.

(*She approaches the KING and speaks confidentially.*)

Only think back to this last night that's passed.

When all around lay buried in deep sleep,

you got up from your bed, and prayed to God.

Send all these here away, and I will tell you

the content of that prayer.

CHARLES: What I confide

to Heaven, need not be concealed from men.

So tell me the content of my prayer, and I

shall doubt no longer you are sent by Heaven.

JOAN: You made three prayers: now, Dauphin, see if I
    can tell you what they were. First, you implored
    Heaven, if any ill-gotten wealth still clung
    to the crown, or any other grievous sin,
    not yet atoned for, dating from the days
    of your forefathers, was responsible
    for stirring up this tragic war, then Heaven
    should take you as a sacrifice for your people,
    and pour the vials of its wrath out on your head alone.
CHARLES: (*Recoiling in fear.*)
    Who are you, prodigy? Where are you from?
    (*All express astonishment.*)
JOAN: You then addressed a second prayer to Heaven:
    that if it was God's will to take away
    the sceptre from your house, and everything
    your fathers, kings before you in this country,
    possessed, you wished to keep three things:
    peace of mind, friendship, and Agnès' love.
    (*The KING hides his face, shaken with sobs; a movement of
    astonishment among all present. A pause.*)
    Shall I tell you what your third prayer was?
CHARLES: No! Enough! I believe in you! No mortal
    could know as much. You are inspired by God.
ARCHBISHOP: Who are you, holy and miraculous girl?
    What blessed country bore you? Speak! Who are
    your parents, whom God has favoured so?
JOAN: My reverend Lord, my name is Joan: I am merely
    the humble daughter of a sheep-farmer,
    from the King's village of Domremy, which lies
    in the bishopric of Toul, and there I've kept
    my father's sheep-flocks, since I was a child.
    I often heard about the islanders
    who'd come across the sea to make us slaves
    and force us to accept a foreign king,
    who did not love our people, and of how
    they had already captured the great city
    of Paris and had conquered all the country.
    I used to pray, in tears, to the Blessed Virgin,

50

to save us from the shame of foreign chains,
and to preserve our true-born king from harm.
Outside the village where I was born there stands
a statue of the Virgin, very old,
where people often come in pilgrimage,
and nearby stands an oak-tree, which is famous
for working miracles: I used to love
to sit in its shadow while I watched the flocks.
And if a lamb got lost upon the hillsides,
a dream would always tell me where it was,
if I slept in the shadow of the oak.
And once, when I had sat a long night through,
under the tree, thinking and praying hard,
and keeping sleep at bay, the Holy Mother
appeared in front of me, carrying a sword
and a flag, but dressed in every other way
like a shepherdess, like me, and she spoke to me:
'Yes, it is me. Rise up, Joan. Leave the flocks.
The Lord has called you to another business.
Take this flag! Put on the sword! With them
go to destroy the enemies of my people!
And lead your King's son on to Rheims, and crown
him with the royal crown!' But I replied:
'How can I bring myself to do such things?
I'm just a girl, I don't know how to fight.'
Then she went on: 'A virgin without stain,
can accomplish all the good deeds in the world,
if she withstands the love that's *of* the world.
Only look at me. I was, like you,
a chaste maid, yet I gave birth to the Lord,
the Lord divine; I am myself divine!'
And then she touched my eyelids, and when I
looked up, the heavens were full of angels,
boys, holding white lilies in their hands,
and there was lovely music in the air.
And so, three nights on end, the Holy One
appeared to me, and called me: 'Rise up, Joan!
The Lord has called you to another business.'

The third night, when she came, then she was angry,
and spoke severely: 'Woman's duty here
on earth is to obey, and patiently
to endure her heavy fate, and purify
herself with constant, unremitting service.
She who has served on earth is great in Heaven.'
And as she spoke, the shepherdess's dress
fell from her, and she stood there, Queen of Heaven,
clad in the brightness of a thousand suns;
then golden clouds lifted her up, slowly
taking her from my sight, to Paradise.
(*Everyone is deeply moved. Agnès SOREL, in tears, hides her
face on the KING's breast.*)

ARCHBISHOP: (*After a long pause.*)
Such heavenly proofs must silence every doubt
that worldly subtlety can cast on them.
Her actions plainly show she speaks the truth,
since God alone can work such miracles.

DUNOIS: I trust her look more than her miracles,
the total innocence of her expression.

CHARLES: And am I, wretched sinner, worthy of
such grace? That eye, unerring and all-seeing,
looks into me and knows my heart is humbled.

JOAN: Humility in great men lights the sky:
you lower yourself, God raises you on high.

CHARLES: And are you saying I shall win this war?

JOAN: I will bring France in tribute to you, Sire.

CHARLES: Orléans is not menaced any more?

JOAN: Sooner expect the Loire to catch on fire.

CHARLES: I'll enter Rheims a conqueror, you say?

JOAN: Though twenty thousand foes should bar the way.
(*All the KNIGHTS present set up a din with their shields and
lances, and show signs of enthusiasm.*)

DUNOIS: Give us the girl to march before us at
the army's head, and we will follow blindly,
wherever she leads us. Her prophetic eye
directs us, and this stout sword shall protect her!

LA HIRE: We shall not fear the world in arms against us,
 if she is at the head of our battalions.
 The God of Victory walks by her side,
 and in the battle she shall be our guide.
 (*The KNIGHTS set up a terrific clatter of weapons and step*
 forward.)
CHARLES: Yes, holy virgin, you shall lead my army:
 its leaders shall obey you. And this sword,
 the emblem of supreme authority,
 which the High Constable of France sent back
 in anger, has now found a worthier hand.
 Take it, holy prophetess, and henceforward…
JOAN: No! Not so, noble Dauphin!
 Not through this instrument of earthly power
 shall my Lord gain the victory. I know
 another weapon by which I shall win.
 Let me describe it as the vision taught me,
 then send to have it brought here.
CHARLES: Go on, Joan.
JOAN: Send to the ancient town of Fierbois,
 there, in Sainte Catherine's churchyard, is a vault,
 where many old iron weapons lie in heaps,
 the spoils of victories of long ago;
 among them is the sword that I must fight with.
 It has three golden lilies stamped along
 its blade: that way it will be recognised.
 Have the sword fetched; it is the one will bring you victory.
CHARLES: Send somebody to do as she commands.
JOAN: And let me carry a white banner, with
 a purple border, and the Queen of Heaven
 and the beautiful Infant Jesus painted on it,
 hovering above the world, for that is how
 the Holy Mother showed me in the vision.
CHARLES: It shall be done, just as you say.
JOAN: (*To the ARCHBISHOP.*)   My Lord,
 lay your priestly hand on my head, and speak
 a blessing on your daughter.
 (*She kneels.*)

ARCHBISHOP: You have come
    to impart a blessing, rather than receive one.
    'Go in the strength of God.' We are unworthy sinners.
    (*JOAN rises.*)
COURTIER: A herald from the English general.
JOAN: Let him come in, for God has sent him here.
    (*CHARLES signs to the COURTIER, who goes out. Enter the*
    HERALD.)
CHARLES: State your commission, Herald.
HERALD: Who is spokesman
    for Charles of Valois, Count of Ponthieu?
DUNOIS: Herald, you are insubordinate.
    Disrespectful boy, have you the gall
    to deny his title to the King of France
    on his own soil? As an ambassador
    you are protected, otherwise –
HERALD: France recognises one king only, and
    that king lives in the English camp.
CHARLES: Be silent, cousin! Your commission, Herald!
HERALD: The noble Lord of Salisbury, aggrieved
    by all the blood that has been shed, and by
    all that shall be shed in the future, is
    holding back his soldiers, with their swords
    still in their scabbards. Now, before Orléans
    is taken by storm, he offers generous terms
    of compromise.
CHARLES: What are they?
JOAN: (*Stepping forward.*)   Sire, allow
    me to reply to him in place of you.
CHARLES: Do so: decide if it will be peace or war.
JOAN: (*To the HERALD.*)
    Who sent you here, and who speaks here through you?
HERALD: The English general, the Earl of Salisbury.
JOAN: That is a lie! He does not speak through you:
    only the living speak, and not the dead.
HERALD: The general is in the best of health,
    and will survive to annihilate you all.

JOAN: He was alive when you last saw him, but
        a shot from Orléans laid him low this morning,
        as he was watching from the observation tower –
        you laugh, because I tell you things that happened
        so far away? If you do not believe
        my words, trust your own eyes. You will overtake
        his funeral upon your homeward journey.
        Now, Herald, say your piece, what is your errand?
HERALD: Since you can tell things which cannot be known,
        you will know what it is before I tell you.
JOAN: I do not need to know your message,
        but you need to know mine, and to take my words
        back to those generals who sent you here.
        – King of England, and you, the Dukes of Bedford,
        and Gloucester, acting as his viceroys,
        make your account to the great King of Heaven
        for all the blood that has been shed by you.
        Surrender all the keys of all the cities,
        which you have taken in defiance of
        the will of Heaven, whose King now sends a virgin
        to offer you peace or bloody war. So choose!
        I tell you now, in order that you know:
        the Son of Mary has not destined France
        to be yours: rather Charles, my Lord and Dauphin,
        to whom God has assigned the kingdom, shall
        enter in royal triumph into Paris,
        attended by the French nobility.
        – Now, Herald, make all speed away from here:
        before you're back in camp to report these scenes,
        I, Joan the Maid, will be already there,
        planting the flag of victory in Orléans.
        (*She goes out, leaving a scene of turmoil.*)

End of Act One.

ACT TWO

Scene 1

A region enclosed by cliffs.
TALBOT and LIONEL, the English commanders. Philip, Duke of
BURGUNDY. The knights FASTOLF and CHATILLON, with soldiers
and standards.

TALBOT: Beneath these cliffs here let us make a halt,
    and pitch a proper camp, and see if we
    can rally our straggling forces once again,
    who fled and scattered at the first alarm.
    Man the heights there, and post reliable guards.
    The night protects us from pursuit: unless
    the enemy has wings as well, I have
    no fear of his attacking. Nonetheless
    we need to use the utmost caution, since
    the enemy is bold, and we've been beaten once.
    (*Exeunt FASTOLF with his men.*)
LIONEL: Beaten! General, do not use that word
    again. I cannot allow myself to think
    how Frenchmen saw the backs of English soldiers
    today. Orléans! Orléans! Grave of our renown!
    England's honour lies slain upon your fields.
    Disgraceful and ridiculous defeat!
    Who will believe it in the years to come?
    The victors of Crécy, Poitiers, Agincourt,
    driven off the field, and by a woman!
BURGUNDY: It must be some small comfort to us that
    we were not beaten by men, but by the devil.
TALBOT: The devil of our own stupidity!
    What, Burgundy, are princes frightened too
    by the same ghosts that terrify the mob?
    Your superstition is a poor disguise
    for cowardice; your troops were first to fly.
BURGUNDY: No one stood fast. It was a general rout.
TALBOT: No, Sir, it was on *your* wing it began.

You all came bursting into our camp, shouting:
'All hell has broken loose – the Devil fights
for France!', and that brought our men to confusion.
LIONEL: You can't deny, your wing was first to break.
BURGUNDY: Only because the first attack was there.
TALBOT: The girl knew just where we were weakest, and
she knew just where to look to find the cowards.
BURGUNDY: So I am to be blamed for this disaster?
LIONEL: If we'd been on our own, the English army,
– by God! – we never would have lost Orléans!
BURGUNDY: Indeed you would not. In that case, you would
never have seen Orléans in the first place.
Who paved the way for you into this country?
held out the hand of friendship to you, when
you set foot on this foreign, hostile coast?
Who crowned your Henry king in Paris? Who
won the hearts of Frenchmen to his side?
By God! Without this strong right arm to lead you,
you wouldn't have seen the smoke from a French chimney.
LIONEL: If great words were great deeds, Duke, you would have
subdued the whole of France all by yourself.
BURGUNDY: You're sulking now, because you lost Orléans,
and have to work your spleen off on your ally.
Why did we lose Orléans? Because of your greed.
The city was prepared to yield to me;
your envy and nothing else prevented it.
TALBOT: We were not laying siege to it for your sake.
BURGUNDY:
And where would you have been, had I withdrawn?
TALBOT: No worse off than at Agincourt, believe me,
when we saw off all France and you as well.
BURGUNDY: Yet you were glad enough to have our friendship;
and the Regent paid a high enough price for it.
TALBOT: Yes, and today the bill fell due for payment;
disgraced, dishonoured, beaten at Orléans.
BURGUNDY: My Lord, you may regret it if you take
this present conversation any further.
Did I desert the standards of my King,

bring down the name of traitor on my head,
to hear such language, from a foreigner?
What am I doing, fighting against my country?
If I must serve the ungrateful, I prefer
to do so for my true and lawful King.

TALBOT: We know you have had secret dealings with
the Dauphin, but we shall find means to shield
ourselves from treachery.

BURGUNDY: Death and damnation!
Am I to be treated in this way?
Chatillon! See my troops prepared to march.
We shall go back to our own country.
(*Exit CHATILLON.*)

LIONEL: *Bon voyage!*
The fame of Englishmen never shone so bright
as when they fought alone, with nothing but
their good stout swords, and no accomplices.
Each man should fight his battle for himself.
This demonstrates the truth of the old saying:
French blood and English don't mix well together.
(*Enter Queen ISABEAU, accompanied by a PAGE.*)

ISABEAU: What am I hearing, generals? Stop this, now!
What baleful planet has disturbed your minds,
and robbed you of your senses in this way?
Will you break out in hatred at a time
when unanimity alone can save us,
and by these broils secure your own destruction?
I beg you, Duke, take back that rash command;
and Talbot, famous as you are, appease
the anger of your ally, and your friend.
Lionel, help me reconcile these fiery spirits.

LIONEL: Not I, my lady; it's all one to me.
In my opinion, what cannot exist
together, should much best be kept apart.

ISABEAU: Do the tricks of Hell, that proved so catastrophic
to us in battle, go on working here,
to fool our senses and confuse our minds?
Who began all this? Speak! My noble Lord –

(To TALBOT.)
did you so far forget your own advantage
as to insult a valuable ally?
What do you think to gain without his aid?
He put your King upon his throne, and keeps
him there, and can remove him at his will.
His troops support your cause, his name still more so.
If every man in England landed on
our coast, they could not overcome this country
if ever it agreed to band together:
no power can conquer France, but France herself.

TALBOT: We know well how to honour our true friends:
to ward off false ones is a wise man's duty.

BURGUNDY: Those who deny the debts of gratitude
are not ashamed to brazen out a lie.

ISABEAU: What was that, noble Duke? Can you forget
your sense of shame and honour so completely
as to extend your hand in friendship to
take the hand that cruelly killed your father?
Are you so mad as to imagine that
the Dauphin ever will be truly reconciled
with the man who drove him to the edge of ruin?
You want to pull him back, so near his fall
and thoughtlessly destroy all you have done?
Your friends are *here*, and your salvation rests
on alliance with England, and on that alone.

BURGUNDY: Peace with the Dauphin had not crossed my mind;
but the contempt and arrogance displayed
by these overbearing English I won't stand.

ISABEAU: Come now! A rash word may be overlooked.
A general has his problems, and ill-fortune
can make a man ill-tempered, as you know.
Come on, embrace! and let me heal this rift
quickly, before it can grow any wider.

TALBOT: Well, Burgundy, what do you say? A noble heart
is always happy to admit the victory
of Reason's arguments. The Queen has spoken
wisely, so let this handclasp heal the wound

my over-hasty words may have inflicted.

BURGUNDY: Madame is right in what she says. My anger,
    however justified, yields to necessity.

ISABEAU: Good! Now seal this newly-made alliance
    with a kiss of brotherhood and may the winds
    carry away the words that have been spoken.
    (*BURGUNDY and TALBOT embrace.*)

LIONEL: (*In an undertone, observing the others.*)
    Much luck attend the peace made by a fury!

ISABEAU: Generals, we have lost one battle. Luck
    was not with us, but do not, for that,
    let your courage falter. If the Dauphin,
    despairing of the aid of God, has called
    Satanic powers into the field, he will
    have sold himself to the Devil all in vain,
    and Hell itself won't be enough to save him.
    His army is led by this victorious girl:
    I shall head yours; *I* shall take the place
    of prophetess and miracle-working virgin.

LIONEL: Madame, go back to Paris. We prefer
    to fight with proper weapons, not with women.

TALBOT: Go! Go! Since you came to our camp,
    nothing but ill-luck has attended us.

BURGUNDY: Yes, go! You do no good by being here;
    the soldiers find your presence here a scandal.

ISABEAU: (*Looks from one to another in astonishment.*)
    You too, Burgundy? Are you taking sides
    against me too with these ungrateful lords?

BURGUNDY: Just go! the men lose heart when they believe
    the cause for which they're fighting might be yours.

ISABEAU: Scarcely have I finished making peace
    between you when you're all in league against me.

TALBOT: Go with God, Madame, but for God's sake, go!
    With you gone, we shall fear no other devils.

ISABEAU: But am I not your true and faithful ally?
    Is not my cause the very same as yours?

TALBOT: Perhaps. But ours is not the same as yours.
    We are engaged in an honourable war.

BURGUNDY: And I avenge my father's bloody murder;
   my cause is sanctified by filial duty.
TALBOT: Let us be frank! What you do to the Dauphin
   cannot be justified to God nor man.
ISABEAU: A curse on him down to ten generations!
   A man who so abuses his own mother!
BURGUNDY: Revenge for both his father and your husband.
ISABEAU: Daring to sit in judgement on my morals!
LIONEL: Tut, tut, such lack of filial respect!
ISABEAU: He had me banished, sent me into exile.
TALBOT: In deference to what the people wanted.
ISABEAU: May I be damned if ever I forgive him!
   Rather than have him rule his father's kingdom…
TALBOT: You'll rather sacrifice his mother's honour!
ISABEAU: You have no notion, poor weak souls, of what
   a mother's heart, once wounded, can accomplish.
   I love whoever does me good, and hate
   whoever does me harm, and if it happens
   that is the son I bore, I hate him worse.
   I gave him life and I can take it back,
   when his proud, ruthless insolence
   stabs at the very womb that carried him.
   You, who are fighting your war against my son,
   have neither right nor reason so to rob him.
   What did the Dauphin ever do to you?
   What promises did he ever break to you?
   Ambition and vulgar envy drive you on.
   I am allowed to loathe him – he is my son.
TALBOT: And he can feel his mother's hand in her revenge.
ISABEAU: You wretched hypocrites, how I despise you.
   You deceive yourselves as much as you do the world.
   You English grasp out greedily for France,
   where you have neither right nor valid claim
   to so much earth as a horse's hoof could cover.
   And this Duke, who so likes to be called 'The Good',
   sells off the country which his fathers left him
   to foreign masters, enemies of France.
   And yet, your every second word is 'Justice'!

How I despise hypocrisy. The way
I am is how I want the world to see me.
BURGUNDY: There's little danger that it won't do that.
ISABEAU: I have warm blood and passions like the next woman.
I came to France to be a queen, not merely
to seem one; was I to give up happiness,
because my carefree youth was cursed by Fate
to be chained to a wretched madman of a husband?
I love my freedom more than life; whoever
wounds me on that point…but what am I doing,
arguing about my rights – with you?
Your blood flows thick and sluggish in your veins;
of pleasure you know nothing, only rage.
And this Duke, who has wavered all his life
between the varied charms of Good and Evil,
can neither love nor hate with real conviction.
I'm going to Melun. Just let me have
this boy – I like the look of him – to keep
me company and amuse me.
(*Pointing to LIONEL.*)   After that
you may do as you like. I have no further
interest in Burgundians or English.
(*She beckons to the PAGE and makes to go.*)
LIONEL: Rely on us to send on to Melun
the prettiest French boys we can take prisoner.
ISABEAU: (*Coming back.*)
You English hack away at everything in sight:
only the French can kill and still remain polite.
(*She leaves.*)
TALBOT: God! What a woman!
LIONEL: Is there a decision
on whether we continue to retreat
or turn and face them, and, by a quick, bold stroke,
wipe out today's disgrace?
BURGUNDY: No, we're too weak;
too scattered, and the men have had no time
to catch their breath after the shock they suffered.

TALBOT: It was blind panic, nothing else, that beat us,
    the swift impression of a moment, and the image,
    so frightening in imagination, seen close to,
    will vanish. Therefore my advice is this,
    to lead the army back at dawn tomorrow,
    against the enemy.
BURGUNDY: Consider though…
LIONEL: With your permission. There is nothing here
    to be considered. We must win back all
    we have lost, and soon, or be disgraced for ever.
TALBOT: It is decided. We attack tomorrow.
    And, to destroy this phantom terror, which
    so dazzles and unmans our troops, let us
    engage this fiendish virgin hand-to-hand.
    If she will meet us, face to face, well then,
    it is the last time she will trouble us:
    if not, and rest assured, she will avoid
    a serious combat, then the spell is broken.
LIONEL: So be it then! and let me be the one
    to fight this easy bloodless tournament.
    I mean to take this ghost alive, and take her
    personally, before the very eyes
    of the Bastard Dunois, her lover, to our camp,
    and let the soldiers have her.
BURGUNDY: Do not promise
    more than you can fulfil.
TALBOT: If ever I get
    my hands on her, I shall not be so gentle.
    Come now, a little sleep. We march at dawn.
    (*Exeunt.*)

Scene 2

JOAN enters, with her flag, wearing helmet and breastplate but otherwise dressed as a woman. DUNOIS, LA HIRE, KNIGHTS and SOLDIERS appear above on the cliff path, and pass silently across it, to reappear immediately afterwards on the stage.

JOAN: (*To the KNIGHTS surrounding her, while the march past above continues.*)

The pass is won, and we are in their camp!
Throw off the secret cover of the night,
which hid your silent march, and with a shout,
tell the enemy you are here in wrath,
give them our battle cry – 'God and the Maid!'
(*A loud cry with a wild clang of weapons.*)
God and the Maid!
(*Trumpets and drums.*)

SENTRIES: (*Offstage.*) The foe! The foe! The foe!

JOAN: Now bring torches! Set their tents on fire!
The fury of the flames will feed their fear,
and death will threaten them from every side.
(*The SOLDIERS rush off; she is about to follow them.*)

DUNOIS: (*Holding her back.*)

Joan, you have done your part now. You have led us
right into their camp, delivered them
into our hand. But now you should withdraw:
leave the arbitrement of blood to us.

LA HIRE: Point us the way to victory, and carry
the flag in front of us in your pure hand,
but do not take the sword yourself to kill,
do not tempt the treacherous god of battles,
for he is blind and merciless with his subjects.

JOAN: Who is there here to hold me back? And who
would dare give orders to my guiding spirit?
The arrow flies where the archer's hand directs it.
Where there is danger is where I must be.
Nor is my fate to die *here*, or *today*:
first I must see the crown on my King's head.
No enemy shall take my life until
I have fulfilled the dictates of God's will.
(*She leaves.*)

LA HIRE: Dunois! Come on then, let us follow her
and lend her all our courage for a shield.
(*Both leave. English TROOPS flee over the stage.*)

A SOLDIER: The maid! Here in the camp!

ANOTHER: Impossible!
How can she be? How can she have got in?
ANOTHER: Through the air. The Devil helped her.
TWO MORE: Run! Run! We're dead men, all of us.
(Exeunt.)
TALBOT: *(Entering.)* They will not hear. I cannot rally them.
All discipline has left them; just as if
the legions of the damned had been spewed out
of Hell, a panic has swept both coward and hero
senselessly off. I cannot find ten men
to throw against the enemy, who floods
into the camp in ever-increasing force.
Am I the only sober man, and all
the rest are raving lunatics? To fly
before these milksop Frenchies, whom we have
trounced in a dozen battles? Who is she,
this invincible goddess of terror, who can turn
the tide of battle all at once, and change
a flock of sheep into a pride of lions?
Could an impostor learn a leading part
so well that she could terrify real heroes?
A SOLDIER: *(Rushing in.)*
General! The Maid! Run!
TALBOT: *(Strikes him down.)*   Run yourself!
To Hell! And any man who speaks of flight
or fear shall have to reckon with my sword.
*(He goes out. The scene opens out till we see the English camp
in flames. Drums, flight and pursuit. After a little while, enter
MONTGOMERY.)*
MONTGOMERY:
Where shall I run to? Death and enemies surround me.
The furious general brandishes his sword to block
our flight and drive us to our deaths, on one side, while
upon the other, she, the terrible Maid, deals death
and rages like a fire! And not a bush to hide me,
not a cave to offer me a place of safety!
Why did I ever have to come across the sea,
miserable fool! I was deceived by an illusion,

to look for cheap and easy fame in the war in France.
Now my ill-luck has brought me to this bloody battle.
I wish I was a long, long way from here, at home,
on the Severn's flowery banks, safe in my father's house,
where I left my mother, weeping, and my girl.
(*JOAN appears in the distance.*)
Oh, God! what do I see! She's there, the horror's coming!
Rising, glowing darkly, out of the flames of fire
like a spirit of the night, out of the jaws of Hell.
Where can I run away to? She holds me in her eyes
of fire already, casting out her net of glances,
unerringly, towards me from far off. My feet
are caught in her snares, tighter and ever tighter,
they refuse to carry me. However much my heart
misgives, I have to look upon that face of death.
(*JOAN takes a few steps towards him, and stops again.*)
She's coming nearer. I'll not wait until the fiend
attacks me first. I shall go on my knees to her,
beg her, implore her for my life – she is a woman –
I have to see if tears have any power to move her.
(*As he starts to go towards her, she advances on him quickly.*)

JOAN: You are a dead man! You were born of an English mother.
MONTGOMERY: (*Falling at her feet.*)
No! Stop! You cannot murder a defenceless man.
I threw away my sword and shield. I am unarmed,
and begging you, falling at your feet, for mercy.
Leave me the light of life, and take a ransom fee.
My father is a rich man, he has property at home,
in Wales, that lovely country, where the silver Severn
snakes through green fields, and fifty villages acknowledge
him as their lord. He will send gold, much gold, to free
a son he loves, if he finds out I'm still alive,
a prisoner of the French.
JOAN: You lost, deluded fool!
You've fallen in the fatal hands of Joan the Maid,
from whom no rescue or escape can be expected.
If Fate had placed you in the power of the tiger,
the crocodile, if you had robbed a lioness of

her cubs, you might have found some pity or compassion.
But there is one way only, for those who meet the Maid.
A terrible contract binds me to the spirit-world,
powerful, invulnerable, and enjoins me
to put to the sword and slaughter every living thing
sent fatally against me by the god of battles.

MONTGOMERY:
Oh, what you say is terrible, but your looks are mild.
You are not frightening at all seen nearer to.
My heart is drawn to you, you are so beautiful,
Oh, by the mildness of your tender sex, I beg you:
have mercy! I am young.

JOAN: Do not invoke my sex!
Do not call me a woman! I have no sex. Like spirits
bodiless, not subjected to the world's ways of loving,
I have no sex, nor does this armour hide a heart.

MONTGOMERY:
Oh, by the holy ruling power of love, which every
heart is subject to, I beg you now to hear me.
I left behind at home, the girl who was to be
my wife, lovely as you, fresh in the charm of youth,
weeping and waiting for her lover to come back.
Oh, if you ever hope to be in love, and hope
your love will be returned, then do not cruelly
divide two hearts that feel the sacred bonds of love.

JOAN: You call upon the alien gods of Earth, whom I
neither worship nor respect. And I know nothing
of all these sacred bonds of love you tell me of;
nor shall I ever recognise its idle power.
Therefore defend yourself; your last hour is at hand.

MONTGOMERY:
Oh, then have mercy on my sorrowing parents, whom
I left behind at home. For you, too, must have parents,
left, sick with worry and concern for you.

JOAN: That was unlucky to remind me of how many
mothers have been made childless here in France,
how many helpless children fatherless, how many
promised brides have been made widows, and through you!

Now let English women experience despair,
and learn to know the tears that have been shed
by France's sorrow-stricken wives and mothers.

MONTGOMERY:
It is hard to die unmourned, and in a foreign land.

JOAN: Who asked you to that land, to lay waste to the crops,
growing in our fields, to drive us from our homes,
to throw the firebrand of war into the peace
and sanctity of our cities? You cherished the illusion
you could reduce the free-born French to abject slavery;
that you could harness this great country, like a dinghy,
behind your mighty man-of-war. Well, you are fools!
The royal arms of France hang near the throne of God:
and you will sooner snatch a star from the Great Bear,
than a village from this country, for it stands eternal,
united, indivisible. The day of vengeance
is near at hand; and you shall not return alive
across that sacred channel God has placed to set
a frontier between our countries, and which you
have blasphemously overstepped.

MONTGOMERY: Oh, I must die!
Death's terror seizes me already.

JOAN: Die, then, friend!
Why timidly draw back from Death, which is the fate
none of us may avoid? Look at me, now. Look!
I am nothing but a girl, a shepherdess by birth,
these hands of mine are quite unused to hold a sword,
they never carried anything more harmful than a crook;
yet, torn away from all the places of my homeland,
my father's arms, my sisters', I must *here*, I *must* –
the voice of Heaven drives me on, not my own will –
rage like an angry spirit, to do you bitter harm,
no joy to me, dealing out death, and at the last,
falling myself a victim to him. I shall not
see the day when I come home again in joy.
I shall bring death to many of you yet, I shall
make many widows still, but, finally, I shall
be killed myself, and so I shall fulfil my destiny.

Now you must fulfil yours. Take up your sword again,
and we shall fight together for the prize of life.

MONTGOMERY: (*Standing.*)
If you are mortal like myself, if weapons can
wound you, perhaps it is my arm that is predestined
to send you down to Hell, and end the woes of England.
I lay my fate in God's all-merciful hand. Now, witch!
Call up your devils to your aid! Fight for your life!
(*He snatches up his sword and shield and attacks her.
Military music sounds in the distance. After a short struggle,
MONTGOMERY falls.*)

JOAN: Your foot was set upon the road to Death – then go there!
(*She moves away from him, and stands, thoughtfully.*)
Oh, Blessed Virgin, you have worked a miracle in me!
You give the strength to my unwarlike arm, and arm
this heart of mine with stern implacability.
My soul melts into pity and my hand draws back,
as if it was encroaching on some holy shrine,
from violating the young bodies of my foes.
I shudder at the very sight of naked steel,
but when the need is there, there also is the strength,
and in my trembling hand, the sword unerringly
moves of its own accord, as if it were alive.
(*Enter a KNIGHT with closed visor.*)

KNIGHT: Damned juggling witch! Your hour has come. All over
the field of battle I have looked for you.
Devil, go back now to the Hell you came from.

JOAN: What man are you, his evil angel sends
to meet me? By your bearing, you could be
a prince; nor do you seem an Englishman,
you wear the insignia of Burgundy,
and against those I shall not raise my sword.

KNIGHT: Degenerate wretch! You do not merit death
at a prince's noble hand. The headsman's axe
should sever your damned head from off your body,
and not the royal sword of Burgundy.

JOAN: So then you are the noble Duke himself?

KNIGHT: (*Raising his visor.*)
I am! Wretched creature, tremble and despair!
your hellish tricks will not protect you now.
Till now you only had to deal with weaklings;
this is a man who faces you.
DUNOIS: (*Entering with LA HIRE.*) Then turn
and fight with men, not women, Burgundy.
LA HIRE: We shall protect the holy prophetess:
your sword will have to run me through before…
BURGUNDY: This ruttish sorceress does not frighten me,
and nor do you, whom she has changed so vilely.
You should blush, Bastard, and you too, La Hire,
for lowering your one-time valour to
the arts of Hell, letting yourselves become
the paltry squires of a devil's trull.
Come on! I challenge all of you. The man
who seeks the aid of Hell, despairs of God.
(*They prepare to fight. JOAN steps in between them.*)
JOAN: Stop!
BURGUNDY: Are you frightened for your lover's life?
Before your very eyes, he shall be…
(*He lunges at DUNOIS.*)
JOAN: Stop!
Part them, La Hire, No French blood must be spilt.
It is not swords that must decide this quarrel.
It has been otherwise decreed above.
Stand apart, I say! Hear and revere
the spirit that enters me, and speaks through me.
DUNOIS: Why do you stay my upraised arm, and why
prevent my sword from settling this in blood?
The steel is drawn, the blow must fall that brings
vengeance and reconciliation to all France.
JOAN: (*Standing between them, and dividing both parties by a wide space, speaks to the BASTARD.*)
Stand over there.
(*To LA HIRE.*)   Don't move from where you are.
I must speak to the Duke.
(*When everyone is quiet.*)   Well, Burgundy?

What is it that you want? Who are these foes
whom you look for with murder in your eyes?
This noble prince is a son of France like you,
this brave man is your countryman and brother
in arms, and I myself a daughter of
your nation. All of us, whom you are trying
to wipe out, we are all one people – yours.
Our arms are spread wide open to receive you;
our knees will gladly bend to do you homage;
our swords will not be raised against you, since
even in enemy uniform, we respect
the royal features we can see in you.

BURGUNDY: Siren! do you intend to lure your victim
with flattery and sweet words to destruction?
Your tricks cannot impose on me. My ears
are stopped to the seductions of your speech,
the armour on my breast is proof against
the fiery arrows darting from your eyes.
Dunois, to arms!
And let us fight with weapons, not with words.

DUNOIS: Words first, then blows. Are you afraid of words?
That is a sort of cowardice as well,
betraying a lack of confidence in your cause.

JOAN: We are not forced to kneel here at your feet,
We do not come to you as suppliants.
Look around! The English camp is burned,
your dead are covering the battlefield,
the drums that you hear beating are French drums:
God has decided, victory is ours.
We are prepared to share the laurels, though,
freshly-plucked as they are, with our friend.
Come over to us! An honourable flight!
Come over to the side of right and victory.
I, who am sent by God, I offer you
a sister's hand, to draw you over to
the side of justice: I shall save you yet.
Heaven sides with France. The angelic host –
although you cannot see them – fight for our King;

the fleur de lys adorns them; like this flag,
our cause is good, and white as purest light:
and its chaste symbol is the Blessed Virgin.

BURGUNDY: The tangled web of lies snares and deceives,
but her speech is just as artless as a child's.
If evil spirits prompt her, they have done
a wonderful counterfeit of innocence.
I will not listen any more. To arms!
I feel my ear is weaker than my hand.

JOAN: You say I am a sorceress, and accuse me
of devil's tricks – is making peace a trick?
disarming hatred an affair of Hell?
Does harmony rise from the infernal regions?
If anything is innocent, good and holy,
is it not surely fighting for one's country?
Since when has Nature been so much at odds
with herself that Heaven would desert
the cause of Right, and devils would defend it?
But if what I have said to you is good,
where would I have it from if not from Heaven?
Who would have to come to me among my flocks,
to teach a simple girl affairs of state?
Princes and kings were strangers to my eyes,
as arts of speech are foreign to my tongue.
But now I need them to convince you, I
possess the insight into higher things.
The fate of kings and empires is now clear
as daylight to my calm, unclouded eyes,
and in my mouth I bear a thunderbolt,

BURGUNDY: (*Deeply agitated, raises his eyes to her, and looks at her
with astonishment and emotion.*)
What's happening to me? Is it a god
that brings about this change of heart in me?
She is not false, if she can move me so.
No! No! If it is magic works on me,
it is the working of a heavenly power;
my heart tells me – she has been sent from God.

JOAN: Look! He is moved! He is! I have not begged
in vain. The thundercloud of anger melts,
and thaws in tears, and from his eyes there shines
the light of peace, the sunlight of emotion.
Put up your swords, and take him to your hearts.
He weeps, we have convinced him, he is ours!
(*Her sword and flag fall from her hands, she hurries over to
him with arms outstretched, and embraces him with passionate
intensity. LA HIRE and DUNOIS lower their swords, and
hasten over to embrace him.*)

End of Act Two.

ACT THREE

Scene 1

The court at Chalons-sur-Marne.

DUNOIS: We have been bosom friends, comrades in arms;
    drawing our swords in common cause, and in
    adversity and death we stayed together.
    Don't let a woman break the bond that has
    outlasted every twist and turn of Fate.
LA HIRE: Prince, listen…
DUNOIS: La Hire! You are in love with Joan.
    I know quite well what you intend to do:
    to go at once to the King and ask him for
    her hand as a reward – he hardly can
    refuse your bravery what it deserves.
    But hear this – rather than see her in the arms
    of someone else, I would…
LA HIRE: Prince, let me speak!
DUNOIS: It's not the superficial pleasure of
    the eye that draws me to her. I had never
    been attracted by a woman; then I saw her,
    the miracle-working girl whom God had sent
    to save the country and to be my wife.
    That was the moment when I swore by all
    that I hold sacred, I would marry her.
    None but the strong deserve the strong: my heart
    burns with a longing to find rest upon
    a kindred bosom which both understands
    and can stand up to all its strength and power.
LA HIRE: I would never dare to weigh my poor deserts
    against the power of your heroic name.
    When Count Dunois enters the lists, then all
    the competition may as well withdraw.
    But can a low-born shepherdess be worthy
    to sit beside you as a wife? Would not
    the royal blood that flows in your veins

disdain to be so shamefully diluted?

DUNOIS: She is a child of God and Nature, just
as I am, and therefore of equal birth.
How could she disgrace a Prince's hand,
she who is wedded to the holy angels,
whose head is haloed with a brighter crown
than any on this earth, who sees the pomp
and circumstance of the world as dross beneath
her feet; pile all the thrones of all the kings
of all the earth on one another, till
they reach the stars, they would not reach the heights
where *she* reigns in angelic majesty!

LA HIRE: Then let the King decide.

DUNOIS: No! She must choose!
She has freed France, she must be free to give
her heart.

LA HIRE: The King!

(*Enter CHARLES, SOREL, DU CHATEL, CHATILLON
and the ARCHBISHOP.*)

CHARLES: You say he's coming here?
To recognise me as his rightful King?

CHATILLON: Here, Sire, in your royal city of Chalons,
the Duke, my master, means to throw himself
in penance at your feet – he ordered me
to greet Your Majesty as lord and King:
and say he follows and will soon be here.

SOREL: He's coming! Oh, the brightness of this day
that brings joy, peace, and reconciliation!

CHATILLON: My Lord will bring two hundred knights with him;
he will kneel down in homage at your feet.
However, he expects that you will *not*
permit that, but will greet him as your cousin.

CHARLES: My heart burns to beat in time with his.

CHATILLON: The Duke requests no mention shall be made
of the old feud at this, your first, encounter.

CHARLES: The past shall be forgotten, and for ever.
We only wish the future to be bright.

CHATILLON: Those who have fought for Burgundy shall be
  included in the general amnesty.
CHARLES: In that way I gain twice as many subjects.
CHATILLON: Queen Isabeau shall also be included
  in this agreement, should she wish to accept it.
CHARLES: She wages war on me, not I on her:
  our fight is over, as soon as she likes to end it.
CHATILLON: Twelve knights shall be hostages for your word.
CHARLES: My word is sacred.
CHATILLON: The Archbishop shall
  divide a sacred host between you both,
  as pledge and seal of reconciliation.
CHARLES: As I hope for salvation at the last,
  my heart and hand are both at one in this.
  What other pledges does the Duke require?
CHATILLON: (*With a glance at DU CHATEL.*)
  There is one person here, whose presence might
  sour the first greeting.
  (*DU CHATEL walks silently away.*)
CHARLES: Go, then, Du Chatel:
  stay hidden till the Duke can bear to see you.
  (*He follows him with his eyes, then hurries over to him and
  embraces him.*)
  My honest friend, you have been more than ready
  to do this and much more to save my peace!
  (*DU CHATEL leaves.*)
CHATILLON: This document explains the other points.
CHARLES: (*To the ARCHBISHOP.*)
  See it is all arranged. We shall agree
  to everything – no price too high for a friend.
  Dunois! take a hundred knights and go
  to meet the Duke and bring him here in friendship.
  The troops must have green branches in their helmets
  to greet their brothers; and the city must
  be decorated for a festival,
  and all the bells shall ring to announce the news
  that France and Burgundy are reconciled.
  (*Enter a PAGE. Trumpets heard off.*)

Listen! What is the meaning of those fanfares?

PAGE: The Duke of Burgundy has made his entrance
   into the court.

   (*Exit.*)

DUNOIS: (*Going out with LA HIRE and CHATILLON.*)
                    Come! Let us go to meet him.

CHARLES: (*To SOREL.*)

   Agnès. you're crying? I too barely have
   the strength to take me through this interview.
   How many had to die to make it possible
   for us to meet in friendship once again!
   But every tempest spends itself at last,
   day follows even the darkest night, and time
   brings ripeness to even the latest fruits.

ARCHBISHOP: (*At the window.*)

   The Duke can hardly force a passage through
   the mob. They've lifted him from off his horse,
   kissing his cloak, his spurs.

CHARLES: A kindly people,
   their love flares up as quickly as their anger.
   They soon forget it was this very Duke
   who massacred their fathers and their sons:
   one moment swallows up a lot of time!
   – Control yourself, Agnès! Excess of joy
   might also prove a thorn in the flesh: I want
   nothing to cause him shame or bitterness.

   (*Enter the Duke of BURGUNDY, DUNOIS, LA HIRE,
   CHATILLON, and two other KNIGHTS of the Duke's entourage.
   BURGUNDY stops at the entrance; the KING goes towards him;
   at the same time, BURGUNDY comes forward, and just as he
   is about to kneel, CHARLES takes him in his arms.*)

   You have surprised us – we had meant to come
   to meet you – but you have the faster horses.

BURGUNDY: Bearing me to my duty.

   (*He embraces SOREL, kissing her on the forehead.*)
                              By your leave,
   cousin: this is the lord's privilege

at Arras, and no pretty woman dares
oppose the custom.
CHARLES: We are told your court
is the seat of Love, the market-place as well,
where all things beautiful are kept in stock.
BURGUNDY: Your Majesty, we are a trading nation,
all that is rich and pleasant from all lands,
comes to the market-place at Bruges to be
displayed for show and use: in value, though,
nothing exceeds the beauty of our women.
SOREL: Surely their fidelity should have
a higher value, if not in the market.
CHARLES: You have a wicked, libellous reputation,
for taking woman's virtue lightly, cousin.
BURGUNDY: Heresy is its own worst punishment.
You are a lucky man, my liege. Your heart
has taught you early, what a dissolute life
has taught me late.
(*He sees the ARCHBISHOP, and gives him his hand.*)
                         Your blessing, Monseigneur.
In the right place, as ever. He who wants
to find you, needs to tread the path of virtue.
ARCHBISHOP: Now let my Maker call me when He will:
my heart is full of joy, I can depart
in peace now, since my eyes have seen this day!
BURGUNDY: (*To SOREL.*)
They say you robbed yourself of all your jewels
to furnish arms against me. Is it true?
Are you so warlike? Was your mind so bent
on my destruction? But our war is over,
all that was lost is found again. Your jewels
have also found their way back to their owner.
You gave them up to ruin me in war:
now take them from my hand, in sign of peace.
(*From one of his attendants he takes a jewel casket and presents
it to her, opened. SOREL looks at the KING in amazement.*)
CHARLES: Take it: a doubly precious gift, a pledge
of love to me and reconciliation.

BURGUNDY: (*Fixing a jewelled rose in SOREL's hair.*)
Why is this not the royal crown of France?
My heart would feel an equal joy to place it
on such a beautiful head.
(*Taking her hand, significantly.*) Rely on me,
if ever you should need a friend!
(*SOREL bursts into tears and steps aside; the KING also struggles to control his feelings; all present watch the two PRINCES with emotion. BURGUNDY, after looking round the whole circle finally throws himself into the KING's embrace.*)
Oh, my dear King!
(*At the same moment, the three Burgundian KNIGHTS hurry forward to embrace DUNOIS, LA HIRE and the ARCHBISHOP. Both PRINCES stand for some time without speaking, in each other's arms.*)
How could I have hated you? How could I
have abandoned you?

CHARLES: Come now, be still, no more.

BURGUNDY: How could I crown that Englishman, and swear
an oath of loyalty to a foreigner!
and all of this to bring about your ruin!

CHARLES: Forget the past! All is forgiven. All
blotted out in a single moment! It
was Destiny, or some unlucky star.

BURGUNDY: (*Grasping his hand.*)
I shall right this wrong: believe me, I shall
make reparation for all you have suffered.
Your kingdom shall be given back to you
entire – not a village will be missing!

CHARLES: We are agreed. I fear no other foe.

BURGUNDY: Believe me, it was with a heavy heart
I took up arms against you. If you knew…
Why did you never send this lady to me?
(*Pointing to SOREL.*)
Those tears of hers I could not have resisted.
No power of Hell can separate us now,
not since we have embraced in brotherhood.

Now I have found out where I need to be,
on this heart all my wanderings have an end.
ARCHBISHOP: (*Stepping between them.*)
Princes, you are united! France arises,
phoenix-like from her ashes, giving promise
of a bright future. The land's grievous wounds
will heal: the villages, the towns that were
destroyed, will rise more splendid from the rubble:
the fields will once again be green. But those
who were the victims of your fatal quarrel,
the dead, will not rise up again: the tears
that have been shed for them cannot be unshed.
The coming generation will be blessed, but not
the one that was the quarry of disaster.
The children's happiness will not wake their fathers.
These are the fruits of war between two brothers!
And let this prove a lesson: fear the god
that dwells within the sword, before you draw it.
The hand of the mighty may unleash a war:
the savage god, though, is not trained to come
like a falcon, back from the skies to the hunter's hand –
he will not come when called. The hand of Heaven
will not save us so punctually twice.
BURGUNDY: My liege! You have an angel by your side.
Where is she? Why do I not see her here?
CHARLES: Where is Joan? Why is she not with us now,
in this high, solemn hour that she made possible?
ARCHBISHOP: She does not like the life of ease at court,
Your Majesty, and when divine command
does not call her to stand before the world,
she modestly avoids the vulgar gaze.
She is certainly in communion with God,
unless she is labouring for France's good,
for Heaven's blessing attends all her footsteps.
(*Enter JOAN, in armour, but without a helmet, wearing a
wreath in her hair.*)
CHARLES: Joan, you appear like a priestess. Have you come
to consecrate the friendship you began?

BURGUNDY: How frightening she was in battle, and
how peace surrounds her with a shining grace!
– Joan! Have I kept my word? Are you content?
Do I not merit your approval now?
JOAN: The greatest good you did was to yourself.
You are now all arrayed in blessed light,
where before all was a gloomy, blood-red glow,
hung like a moon of terror in the sky.
(*She looks about.*)
I see assembled here a number of
noble knights, whose eyes all shine with joy,
only one sorrowful one have I encountered,
who has to hide himself, while all rejoice.
BURGUNDY: And who is conscious of such heavy guilt
that he despairs of winning our goodwill?
JOAN: May he approach? Oh, tell me that he may!
Make your reform complete. It cannot be
called reconciliation, where the heart
is not entirely freed. One drop of hatred
left in the cup of joy turns all to poison.
However black the crime, let Burgundy
forgive it on this day of celebration,
BURGUNDY: Your drift is getting clearer.
JOAN: Will you forgive him?
You will, Duke? – Come in, Du Chatel!
(*She opens the door and leads in DU CHATEL, who stops some
distance away.*)
The Duke is reconciled to all his enemies,
you too.
BURGUNDY: What are you doing to me, Joan?
Are you aware of what it is you're asking?
JOAN: A generous master opens his doors to all,
there is no guest that he shuts out. A pardon,
free as the firmament above the earth,
should not distinguish between friend and foe.
The sun's rays are sent out alike to each
and every corner of infinity;
the sky drops dew in equal measure on

all living things that thirst. All that is good,
all that comes from above belongs to all,
without reserve: but darkness dwells in corners.
BURGUNDY: Oh, she can twist and bend me as she pleases.
My heart turns to soft putty in her hands.
– Du Chatel! Come! Embrace me. I forgive you.
Ghost of my father, do not scold, if I
now take in friendship the hand that struck you down.
Gods of death, do not hold it against me,
if I now break my solemn vow of vengeance.
Down in your home of everlasting night,
no heart beats any more; all is eternal,
fixed, motionless. But up here, in the sunlight,
it is different: Man lives, and feels, and is
the easy prey of the tremendous moment.
CHARLES: (*To JOAN.*)
What is there I do not have you to thank for?
Marvellous girl! How well you kept your word!
How quickly you reversed my destiny,
reconciled me with my friends, and threw
my enemies down into the dust, and freed
my cities from the foreign yoke! You alone
accomplished this. How am I to reward you?
JOAN: Be as humane in your prosperity
as in adversity – and on the summit
remember the value of a friend in need,
which you have learned in times of degradation.
Do not refuse the meanest of your subjects
justice and mercy; it was from the sheepfolds
that God called your deliverer. You will
unite all France beneath your rule, and be
the father of a mighty line of kings;
those who come after you shall shine more brightly
than those who have preceded you on the throne.
The line will flourish, just as long as it
retains the love its people feel for it.
All that can bring it to a fall is pride:
from the mean huts from which salvation came

to you today, mysterious destruction
threatens the guilty scions of your house.
BURGUNDY:
You whom the voice of Heaven inspires to prophecy,
if you can see into the womb of time,
speak to me also of my dynasty. Will it
continue in the splendour it began in?
JOAN: Duke, you have raised your seat as high as a throne,
and your proud heart would raise it higher still,
to lift the whole bold structure to the clouds.
But a higher power will suddenly halt its growth.
Do not for that, though, fear your house's fall.
It will live on in splendour through a daughter,
and sceptred kings, the shepherds of their people,
will issue from her. They shall sit upon
twin thrones of power, and hand down laws to all
the known world, and to another, newer world,
that God still hides across uncharted seas.
CHARLES: Tell us, now, if the Spirit will reveal it,
will this alliance we have just renewed,
also unite our children and grandchildren?
JOAN: (*After a pause.*)
You – Kings and rulers! Have a care of discord!
Do not wake the spirit of dissension,
now sleeping in its lair, for, once aroused,
it will not easily be tamed again.
It will beget a brood of iron children,
and from one firebrand, light one after another.
– Demand to know no further, but enjoy
the present, while I silently conceal
the shape of things to come.
SOREL: Oh, holy maid,
you see into my heart. You know if it
is vainly seeking greatness. Give me too
a welcome prophecy.
JOAN: The spirit shows
me only the mighty happenings in the world.
Your destiny is contained in your own breast.

DUNOIS: Exalted and beloved of God, what will
　　　your destiny be? All happiness on earth
　　　should be hers, who is holiness itself.
JOAN: Happiness dwells with my eternal Father.
CHARLES: Your happiness is henceforth your King's concern:
　　　for I shall make your name great through all France,
　　　all future generations shall call thee blessed.
　　　This shall be done at once! Kneel down!
　　　(*He draws his sword and touches her with it.*) Now, rise:
　　　a noblewoman! I, your king, here raise you
　　　out of the dust and darkness of your birth –
　　　your forbears I ennoble in their graves –
　　　your coat of arms shall bear the fleur-de-lys,
　　　and you shall be the equal of the best
　　　in France: none but the blood of Valois shall
　　　be held superior to yours. The greatest
　　　of all my subjects shall feel honoured by
　　　your hand, and it shall be my first concern
　　　to fit you with a worthy, noble husband.
DUNOIS: (*Stepping forward.*)
　　　My heart chose her already, when she was
　　　nothing: this latest honour does her justice,
　　　but changes neither her merits or my love.
　　　Here in the presence of my sovereign and
　　　this holy bishop, I do offer her
　　　my hand, to be my noble consort, if
　　　she thinks me worthy to make such an offer.
CHARLES: Wonder on wonder! Now I must believe
　　　that nothing is impossible to you:
　　　if you can bring this stubborn heart to heel,
　　　which always scorned the universal power
　　　of Love, until this moment.
LA HIRE: (*Stepping forward.*)   But her brightest
　　　ornament, if I understand her right,
　　　is modesty of heart. She well deserves
　　　the homage of the great, but she will never
　　　raise her desires so high. She does not strive
　　　to reach the dizzy peaks of earthly grandeur.

She is contented with the true affection
of an honest heart, and with the tranquil lot
which I here offer to her, with my hand.
CHARLES: La Hire, you as well! Two noble claimants,
one famous and heroic as the other!
You reconcile my enemies, unite
my kingdom, now you want to part my friends?
Well, only one of them can have her: since
in my judgement, both are worthy of her,
then she must speak herself, her heart must choose.
SOREL: (*Coming closer.*) The noble maid is taken by surprise,
I see the blood rush to her modest cheeks.
Let her have time to ask her heart the question:
unburden herself to a friend of her own sex,
and break the seal still on her tight-locked breast.
Now is the moment even I may be
allowed to go to this unbending girl,
and offer her the confidence of a sister.
Let women first talk over women's matters,
and wait and see what we decide.
CHARLES: So be it!
(*He starts to leave.*)
JOAN: No! Sire, not so! The reason why I blushed
was not the confusion of some silly shame.
I've nothing to confide to this great lady
I'd be ashamed to say in front of men.
These noble men have honoured me in their choice,
but I did not give up a shepherd's life, to gain
an empty, high position in the world.
Nor did I put on armour, so that I
could braid a bridal wreath into my hair.
It is a different mission I am called to,
and one which only a virgin can complete.
I am a soldier of the Lord of Hosts:
I cannot be the wife of any man.
ARCHBISHOP: Woman was made for man, to be his loving
companion, and she best serves the will
of God, if she obeys the voice of Nature.

When you have carried out sufficiently
your God's commands upon the battlefield,
then you will lay aside your arms and come
back to the gentler sex you have denied,
unsuited to the bloody work of war.

JOAN: Most reverend Father, I cannot yet say
what the Spirit will order me to do:
but when the time comes, it will not be silent,
and I shall do its bidding. For the moment,
it bids me to complete my work. My Lord
is not yet crowned: the sacred oil has not
been poured upon his head, nor does my Lord
yet bear the title of the King of France.

CHARLES: Our feet are set upon the road to Rheims.

JOAN: We cannot loiter while the enemy
is still on the alert to intercept us.
But I shall lead you on through all of them!

DUNOIS: But when it is all over, and complete,
when we have entered Rheims victorious,
then, oh, most holy maiden, will you let me…

JOAN: If it is Heaven's will that I come back
victorious from this mortal struggle, then
my work will be done – the shepherdess will have
no further business in her sovereign's house.

CHARLES: (*Taking her hand.*)
It is the Spirit's voice that moves you now,
silencing Love in the heart that God has filled,
But believe me, it will not be quiet for ever!
Weapons will be laid aside, and victory
will lead Peace by the hand, and joy return
to every heart, and gentler feelings wake
in every breast – in yours as well – and you
will shed tears of sweet unfulfilled desire,
such as you never shed before: that heart
which Heaven alone now fills to overflowing,
will turn in love towards a mortal lover.
Your rescuing arm has rendered thousands happy:
you will, at last, bring happiness to *one*.

JOAN: Dauphin! Are you so tired already of
the visible presence of God, you seek to smash
the vessel that contains it, and drag down
into the dust, the virgin God has sent you?
Oh, ye of little faith! Your hearts are blind!
The majesty of Heaven shines around you:
its miracles are done before your eyes:
and you see nothing in me but a woman.
Well, is it womanly to strap on armour
and meddle in the male preserve of war?
And woe betide me if I took God's sword
of vengeance in my hand, while in my heart
I bore an idle passion for some man!
Better for me, if I had not been born!
Not one word more of this, I tell you, if
you do not wish to see the spirit in me
roused to a fury. Any man who looks
at me with longing is a horror to me,
a sacrilege.
CHARLES: Enough! There is no point in trying to move her.
JOAN: Give the command to sound for the attack.
This cease-fire frightens and depresses me;
it rouses me out of this idle rest,
to see my mission done, recalling me
to put my destiny to the final test.
(*Enter a KNIGHT in haste.*)
CHARLES: What is it?
KNIGHT: The enemy has crossed the Marne,
and drawn his army up in line of battle.
JOAN: Battle and War! Now my soul's fetters fall.
To arms! I shall see the army marshalled.
(*She hurries out.*)
CHARLES: La Hire, go with her – they mean to make us fight
for the crown to the gates of Rheims itself.
DUNOIS: It is not real courage drives them, but
the last throw of a frantic, faint despair.
CHARLES: I do not spur you, cousin Burgundy.
Today atones for many evil days.

BURGUNDY: You will have no complaint of me.

CHARLES: I shall
    march at your head along the road to glory,
    and at the coronation city, fight
    for a crown. – Agnès! your knight bids you farewell.

SOREL: (*Embraces him.*)
    I shall not weep for you, nor tremble for you.
    My faith is firmly placed up in the clouds;
    So many signs and pledges of Heaven's grace
    are not vouchsafed to end in grief and pain.
    My conquering lord I shall again embrace
    – my heart tells me – when Rheims is ours again!
    (*Trumpets sound an energetic flourish, which changes, during
    the scene-change, to wild, discordant battle-music. As the next
    scene starts, the music strikes up accompanied by an offstage
    military band.*)

Scene 2

*The scene changes to an open space, bordered by trees. During the opening
music, SOLDIERS can be seen, swiftly retreating in the background.
TALBOT enters, leaning on FASTOLF, accompanied by SOLDIERS.*

TALBOT: Put me down here now, underneath these trees,
    and take yourselves back to the battle. I
    do not need anybody's help to die.

FASTOLF: This is a terrible, unhappy day!
    (*Enter LIONEL.*)
    Oh, what a sight you find here, Lionel:
    the general is mortally wounded.

LIONEL: God forbid!
    My Lord, stand up, this is no time for weakness.
    Do not give in to Death, use your iron will
    to order Nature to revive in you!

TALBOT: No use! The day has come when it is fated
    that we should lose the throne we held in France.
    I have staked our last strength in a desperate fight
    to avert this fate, but it has been in vain.
    And I lie here, struck to the ground by steel,

I shall not rise again – and Rheims is lost;
now hurry to save Paris.
LIONEL: Paris has signed a treaty with the Dauphin:
a courier came just now bringing the news.
TALBOT: (*Tearing off his bandages.*)
Then let the rivers of my blood flood out,
for I am tired of looking at this sun.
LIONEL: I cannot stay here – Fastolf, take the general
to somewhere safe, we cannot hold our present
position: the men are flying on all sides.
The Maid is pressing forward, unopposed.
TALBOT: The triumph of folly, and the death of me!
With idiocy the gods themselves contend
in vain. Reason, exalted, and sublime,
bright-rayed daughter, sprung from the head of God,
the wise ordainer of the universe,
the steerer of the stars, who are you then,
when, tied to the tail of the maddened horse of Frenzy,
calling out unavailingly, you see
yourselves hurled down together to the pit?
Damn all of those who spend their lives pursuing
the great, the worthy, and whose noble minds
are spent in well-laid plans. The King of Fools
is lord of *this* world…
LIONEL: General, you have
not much time left – think of your Maker now!
TALBOT: If we had been brave men, and had been beaten
by other brave men, we could have found comfort
in the common fate of all men, and the turns
of Fortune on her wheel – but to have been
conquered by such vulgar conjuring tricks!
Was all our serious and hard-working life
not worthy of a more imposing exit?
LIONEL: (*Giving him his hand.*)
My lord, goodbye. The tears I owe you shall
be paid in full after the battle's over,
assuming I am still alive to pay them.
But now the fate that sits above the field

in judgement, handing down men's destinies,
summons me too. We meet in another world:
so short a parting for so long a friendship.
(*He goes out.*)

TALBOT: Soon it will all be over; I shall give
back to the earth, the everlasting sun,
those atoms which made up my joy and sorrow –
and of the mighty soldier Talbot, whose
great fame once filled the world, there will be nothing
but a little handful of dust – so a man dies.
And all the profit we can reap from this
struggle of life is insight into…nothing,
and cordial contempt for everything
that we thought noble and desirable…
(*Enter CHARLES, BURGUNDY, DUNOIS, DU CHATEL,
and TROOPS.*)

BURGUNDY: We have taken the redoubt.

DUNOIS: The day is ours.

CHARLES: (*Noticing TALBOT.*)
See who that is over there who bids so hard
and unwilling a farewell to the light of day?
His armour shows he is no common soldier.
Give him some help, if help is still to give.
(*SOLDIERS step forward.*)

FASTOLF: Get back! And stand away! Respect the death
of a man you never came near when alive.

BURGUNDY: What do I see? Talbot, covered in blood!
(*He goes towards him, TALBOT stares at him unblinkingly
and dies.*)

FASTOLF: Get away, Burgundy! A hero's dying eyes
should not be pained by looking at a traitor!

DUNOIS: The Talbot we so feared! The invincible!
Are you content with such a little ground
for whom the whole of France was not enough
to satisfy your spirit's great ambition?
Now, for the first time, Sire, I call you King,
the crown still sat uneasily on your head
as long as there was still breath in this body.

CHARLES: (*After looking silently at the dead man.*)
    A higher power has struck him down, not we.
    He lies upon the soil of France, just like
    a hero on the shield he would not leave.
    Take him away!
    (*SOLDIERS lift the corpse and carry it out.*)
                        And peace be with his dust!
    He shall be given a monument of honour.
    Here, in the midst of France, where his career
    as hero ended, there his bones will rest.
    No enemy advanced as far as he;
    the place he died shall be his epitaph.
FASTOLF: (*Giving up his sword.*)
    My Lord, I am your prisoner.
CHARLES: (*Giving it back.*)   Not at all!
    Such duties are respected even in war.
    Follow your master to the grave in freedom.
    Du Chatel, hurry to Agnès, relieve her
    of the anxiety with which she trembles for us.
    Tell her we are victorious and alive,
    bring her to Rheims in triumph!
    (*Enter LA HIRE.*)
DUNOIS: La Hire!
    Where is the Maid?
LA HIRE: I might ask that of you.
    I left her fighting at your side.
DUNOIS: I thought
    she was protected by your troops, when I
    hurried away to give the King assistance.
BURGUNDY: I saw her banner waving in the thick
    of the enemy forces not so long ago.
DUNOIS: Oh, God, where is she? I feel a foreboding
    of ill. Come, we must save her. I'm afraid
    her courage may have taken her too far,
    and that she fights alone, hemmed in all round,
    she may fall victim to sheer weight of numbers.
CHARLES: Save her!
LA HIRE: I am with you.

BURGUNDY: So are we all!
   (*They rush out.*)

Scene 3

Another desolate part of the battlefield. In the distance, the towers of Rheims can be seen in the sunlight. A KNIGHT appears, entirely in black armour with a closed visor. JOAN pursues him to the front of the stage, where he halts and stands, waiting for her.

JOAN: Creature of tricks! I can see through them now.
   Deceitfully, by counterfeited flight
   you have enticed me from the battlefield,
   saving so many British boys from death and destiny.
   But fate has finally caught up with you.
THE BLACK KNIGHT:
   Why do you dog me in this way, and cling
   so furiously to my heels? It is not
   your hand by which it is my fate to die.
JOAN: I hate you from the bottom of my soul,
   creature of night, whose colour is your own
   An overmastering desire impels me
   to blot you out utterly from the light of day.
   Who are you? Put your visor up. Had I
   not seen the warlike Talbot fall in battle,
   I could well be persuaded you were Talbot.
THE BLACK KNIGHT:
   Do your prophetic voices tell you nothing?
JOAN: They speak aloud within my very heart
   to tell me that misfortune stands before me.
THE BLACK KNIGHT: Joan of Arc! Up to the gates of Rheims
   you have pressed forward on the wings of victory.
   Now let the fame you've won be enough for you.
   Dismiss the fortune that has served you as
   your slave, before it frees itself in anger.
   It has no love of loyalty, and serves
   nobody to the end.
JOAN: What do you mean,
   to halt me in mid-career, my work half-done?

I shall complete it, and fulfil my vow.

THE BLACK KNIGHT:

All-powerful creature, nothing can withstand you;
you have won every battle: but do not
attempt to fight another. Hear my warning!

JOAN: I shall not let my sword sleep in my hand,
till England's pride lies vanquished in the dust.

THE BLACK KNIGHT:

Look over there! There rise the towers of Rheims,
the goal you fought for and your journey's end.
The vast cathedral glitters in the light,
which you will enter in triumph, and where you
will crown your King, and so fulfil your vow.
Do not go in there! Turn back! Hear my warning!

JOAN: What creature are you, double-tongued and false,
trying to frighten me and to confuse me?
How do you dare commit the treachery
of bringing me false prophecies?
(*The BLACK KNIGHT makes to go, but JOAN steps across his path.*)   No! stay
and answer me, or perish at my hands!
(*She is about to aim a blow at him.*)

THE BLACK KNIGHT: (*Touches her with his hand; she stands motionless.*)
Kill what can be killed!
(*Darkness, thunder and lightning. The BLACK KNIGHT sinks out of sight.*)

JOAN: (*Stands amazed at first, but soon recovers herself.*)
That was no living creature – an illusion
of Hell is what it was, or some rebellious
demon that came up from the pit of fire
to shake my steadfast heart from its foundations.
Armed with the sword of God, who should I fear?
I shall complete my task victorious.
And should they summon all the hosts of Hell
to fight for them, my courage shall not fail.
(*She starts to go Enter LIONEL.*)

LIONEL: Turn, you damned witch, turn and prepare to fight.
Both of us shall not leave this place alive.
The best men of my people you have killed,
the noble Talbot breathed out his great soul
here in my arms, and I shall have revenge
for him, or if not, share his destiny.
And so that you may know who brings you fame
whether he wins or dies – my name is Lionel,
last of our army's princes, and unconquered.
(*He attacks her. After a short fight she knocks the sword out of his hand.*)
Damn my ill-fortune!
(*He struggles with her. JOAN seizes him from behind by the crest of his helmet and pulls the helmet violently off, so that his face is exposed, at the same time brandishing her sword in her right hand.*)

JOAN: Die as you would have killed!
The Blessed Virgin kills you now, through me!
(*At this moment she looks him in the face; the sight affects her: she stands without moving, then slowly lets her arm fall.*)

LIONEL: Why do you hesitate? Why do you not strike?
You've killed my fame, now take my life as well.
I am in your hands, and I ask no quarter.
(*She gestures to him to escape.*)
Escape? Owe my life to you? I prefer death!

JOAN: (*Her face turned away.*)
Save yourself! I do not want to think
your life was in my power.

LIONEL: I hate both you,
and what you offer. I do not want mercy.
Now kill the enemy who detests you, and
who would have killed you.

JOAN: Kill me, then – and run!

LIONEL: Ha! What is this?

JOAN: (*Hiding her face.*)   Alas!

LIONEL: They say you kill
all Englishmen you take in battle. Why
are you sparing only me?

JOAN: (*Raises her sword to him suddenly, but lowers it again quickly, as she looks into his face.*) Oh, Holy Virgin!

LIONEL: Why call on her? She does not know you. Heaven is ignorant of you.

JOAN: (*In the most violent anxiety.*) What have I done? My vow is broken!
(*She wrings her hands in despair.*)

LIONEL: (*Looks at her with sympathy, and goes up to her.*)
                     Poor unhappy girl!
I'm sorry for you. And I'm touched. You showed
magnanimity to me alone.
I feel my hatred vanishing, and all
I know is that I feel compassion for you.
Who are you? Where do you come from?

JOAN: Go away!
Make your escape!

LIONEL: I feel compassion for
your beauty and your youth. The sight of you
strikes to my heart. I want so much to save you.
How can I do it? Tell me how? Come! Come!
Abandon this appalling covenant –
throw down your weapons.

JOAN: I am no longer worthy
to carry them.

LIONEL: Then throw them down now, quickly,
and follow me!

JOAN: (*With horror.*) Follow you?

LIONEL: Yes. You can be saved.
Follow me, and I will save you, but
no more delay. I feel unutterable
sorrow for you, a nameless longing for
your safety…
(*He lays hold on her arm.*)

JOAN: Here comes the Bastard! Yes! They're looking for me.
If they should find you here…

LIONEL: I shall protect you!

JOAN: If you die at their hands, I should die too.

LIONEL: Then you do feel for me?

JOAN: Oh saints in Heaven!
LIONEL: Shall I see you again? Or hear from you?
JOAN: No! Never!
LIONEL: This sword shall be my guarantee
    of seeing you again.
    (*He snatches her sword from her.*)
JOAN: How dare you! You are mad!
LIONEL: Now I must yield to force, but we shall meet again!
    (*He goes out. Enter DUNOIS and LA HIRE.*)
LA HIRE: It is her! She's alive!
DUNOIS: Joan: have no fear.
    Your friends are here and powerful at your side.
LA HIRE: Was that not Lionel?
DUNOIS: Let him escape.
    Joan, the cause of righteousness has triumphed.
    The gates of Rheims are opened, and all the people
    are cheering and running out to meet their King.
LA HIRE: What is the matter? She's gone white: she's fainted!
    (*JOAN staggers and is about to fall.*)
DUNOIS: She has been wounded – take her armour off –
    it's on her arm: a superficial wound.
LA HIRE: There's quite a lot of blood.
JOAN: Oh, let my life
    stream forth with it!
    (*She lies unconscious in LA HIRE's arms.*)

End of Act Three.

ACT FOUR

Scene 1

A festively decorated hall, the pillars festooned; offstage the sound of flutes and oboes.

JOAN: The storm of war is hushed: now far and wide
    singing and dancing follow the bloody fight.
    Streets hum with riot: arms are laid aside:
    green branches rear themselves, and stand upright
    to make triumphal arches: columns are tied
    with garlands, while the churches blaze with light.
    The whole of Rheims cannot make room for all
    the guests who flood in to the festival.

    One joy, one thought, one feeling lights a flame
    in every heart, and all those who of late
    were enemies, now happily exclaim
    in general joy, who once felt partial hate.
    And every man who says he bears the name
    of Frenchman, feels a pride in his estate.
    New glory shines about the ancient crown,
    as France pays homage to her royal son.

    But I, who brought these glorious things about,
    I have no part in this festivity.
    My heart is changed, and turned quite inside out,
    my eyes gone over to the enemy.
    From all this happiness my heart takes flight,
    and in the English camp finds sanctuary.
    Out of the happy circle I must tread
    to hide the guilt that laps my heart like lead.

    Who? I? Is the image of a man
    fixed in this pure heart of mine?
    Filled with Heaven's grace, how can
    it beat with love less than divine?
    Warrior at God's right hand,
    I brought salvation to my land:

now I love an enemy,
there, where the chaste sun may see,
why am I not destroyed by shame?
(*The music behind the scene changes to a soft, melting tune.*)
Oh, the pain! The pain! That music!
Every note strikes on my ear,
calling up his voice, his face,
as if he stood before me here.
Just to be back in the battle,
weapons hissing all around:
in the fury of the war,
courage could once more be found.

But these voices and this music,
setting snares about my heart!
All the strengths I have inside me
melt in impotence and turn
to melancholy tears that burn.
(*After a pause, she goes on with greater animation.*)
Should I have killed him? Could I – once I had
looked into his eyes? *Then* kill him? I would sooner
have turned the murdering sword upon myself.

Must I be punished then, for being human?
Is pity sinful? Pity! Did you hear
the voice of pity and humanity
with all those others, victims of your sword?
The Welshman – why was Pity silent then? He was
only a boy, and begging for his life.
The heart is cunning, and can lie to Heaven:
it was not pity by which you were driven.

Why did I have to look into his eyes?
And see the noble outlines of his face?
It was with seeing that your crime began.
Poor wretch! God asks for blind obedience in His tools:
you must be blind to do His bidding well,
Once you had seen, His shield was taken away;
you were entangled in the snares of Hell.
(*The flutes begin again; she falls into a silent melancholy.*)

My shepherd's crook! Would I had never
exchanged it for a sword, nor heard
in the sacred oak tree's branches,
rustling, the holy word.
Mary, Mother, Queen of Heaven,
would you never had come down;
take away what I could never
have deserved, your holy crown.

I have seen the heavens open,
and the blessèd, face to face.
But on earth is all my hoping,
and in Heaven I've no place.
Why did you have to charge me with
this dreadful task I must fulfil?
Must I then deny a heart
that's framed to feel, and by God's will?

If you must display your might,
choose those who, in heavenly light,
and free from sin, dwell all about
your eternal mansion. Send them out
who are immortal, sinless, pure,
who neither pain nor grief endure:
but do not send the shepherd maid,
the weak of soul, the sore afraid.

What did I care for the wars?
Were prince's quarrels my concern?
Free from guilt I grazed my lambs
on the silent mountain heights.
But you tore me from that life,
brought me to the royal hall,
gave me up to guilt and strife.
Oh! The choice – not mine at all!
(*Enter Agnès SOREL in great agitation. As she catches sight of
JOAN, she hurries over to her, and falls about her neck. Suddenly
she recollects herself, lets JOAN go, and kneels in front of her.*)
SOREL: No! Here in the dust in front of you…
JOAN: (*Trying to raise her up.*)   Get up!

What is this? You forget yourself, and me.

SOREL: Let me! It is excess of joy that throws
    me down here at your feet. I must pour out
    my overflowing heart to God: it is in you
    I worship the invisible. You are
    the angel who led my lord to Rheims, and put
    the crown upon his head. What I had never
    thought to see even in dreams, has come to pass.
    The coronation ceremonial
    is ready, the King waits in his robes of state,
    the peers and the grandees are all convened
    to bear the royal insignia, and the crowd
    pours in a wave towards the great cathedral,
    where dances sound, and all the bells ring out!
    This happiness is more than I can bear!
    (*JOAN raises her gently. Agnès SOREL is silent for a moment,*
    as she peers closely into the MAID's eyes.)
    But you are still so serious and austere;
    you are the cause of happiness in others,
    but cannot share in it. Your heart is cold,
    you do not feel our joys: your eyes have seen
    the glory of the Lord, and your pure heart
    is not stirred by our earthly happiness.
    (*JOAN seizes her hand violently, but lets her go again quickly.*)
    Could you not be a woman, feel like one?
    Take your armour off, the wars are done,
    confess you are one of the gentler sex.
    My loving heart draws back in fear from you,
    while you are still the stern chaste goddess of war.

JOAN: What do you want of me?

SOREL: Lay down your arms!
    And take this armour off. Love fears to come
    too near this heart that is encased in steel.
    Oh, be a woman, and you will know love!

JOAN: Take off my armour now? Just now? I would
    sooner fight battles naked and unarmed.
    Not now! May sevenfold steel protect me
    both from these celebrations – and myself.

SOREL: Count Dunois loves you, and his generous heart,
    only susceptible to fame and heroism,
    now glows with a holy flame for you as well.
    It is so fine to be loved by a hero;
    but finer still to love one!
    (*JOAN turns away disgusted.*) But you hate him!
    No, it is merely that you cannot love him.
    What reason could you ever have to hate him?
    We only hate those who have robbed us of
    the ones we love, and there is none you love.
    Your heart is calm – if it could only feel…
JOAN: Have pity on me, and on my destiny.
SOREL: But what is lacking now to make you happy?
    You have done what you promised. France is free,
    and you have brought the King, victorious,
    to the coronation city. You have won
    fame for yourself; a happy nation does
    you reverence and homage; all tongues speak
    in praise of you; you are the goddess of
    this celebration, and the King himself,
    despite his crown, shines not so bright as you.
JOAN: I wish the earth would open up and swallow me!
SOREL: What is this? What has caused these strange emotions?
    Who can hold his head high on this day,
    if you look downcast? I am the one to blush –
    I, who compared to you, feel I am worthless;
    I, who could never measure up to your great deeds,
    your loftiness. Shall I confess my weakness?
    It is not the glory of the fatherland,
    nor the renewed distinction of the throne,
    nor yet the people's joy in victory
    moves this weak heart of mine. There is only one,
    who occupies it utterly; it has no room
    for more than this one, palpable emotion:
    He is the loved of all, it is for Him
    the people shout, on Him they shower their blessings,
    it is in His path that they scatter flowers:
    my beloved is mine, and truly. I am His.

JOAN: Count yourself blessed! You are so fortunate
    to love where all love! You may lay your heart
    wide open, speak aloud of your delight,
    display it in the face of all the world.
    This national festival is the festival
    of your love: all those people flooding in
    in countless numbers into the town – they share
    your feelings, their communion consecrates them
    it is for you they shout, make wreaths and dance,
    you are at one with the universal joy,
    you love what brings delight to everyone,
    the sun; all you can see is your Love's splendour!
SOREL: (*Falling on her neck.*)
    Oh, you have understood me utterly!
    I am so glad. I was mistaken in you.
    You do know what love is; you express my feelings
    so powerfully, my heart is freed from fear
    and shyness, and goes out to you in trust…
JOAN: (*Violently disengaging herself from her embrace.*)
    Leave me alone! Don't touch me! You will be
    infected by the presence of the plague!
    Go and be happy. Leave me to hide my guilt,
    my wretchedness, my fear, in night and darkness…
SOREL: You're frightening me: I do not understand you.
    But I could never understand – your dark,
    mysterious nature always remained hidden.
    Could anyone understand what terrifies
    your holy heart, your pure and tender soul?
JOAN: You are the holy one! You are the pure one here!
    If you could see into my heart, you would
    push me away in horror, as a traitress
    and an enemy.
    (*Enter DUNOIS, LA HIRE and DU CHATEL with JOAN's
    flag.*)
DUNOIS: We were looking for you, Joan.
    Everything's ready, the King sends us to say
    he wants you to carry the holy flag before him.
    You are to join the cortège of the Princes,

and take the last place, closest to himself.

He does not deny, and all the world shall know

that this day's honour is due to you alone.

JOAN: I am to walk in front of him? Carry the flag?

DUNOIS: Who else is suitable? What other hand

is pure enough to bear the holy relic?

You waved it in the battle, carry it now,

to dignify the joy of this procession.

(*LA HIRE is about to hand her the flag but she draws back with a shudder.*)

JOAN: No! No! Take it away!

LA HIRE: What is the matter?

Frightened of your own flag? Look at it now!

(*He unfurls the banner.*)

It is the same one that you waved in triumph.

Here is the picture of the Queen of Heaven

floating above the earth, just as you said

the Holy Mother had instructed you.

JOAN: (*Looking at it in horror.*)

It is! It's her! As she appeared to me.

See how she looks at me and frowns in anger

burning from under those dark eyelashes.

SOREL: She is beside herself! Come to your senses.

It's nothing real that you're looking at:

it's just a picture, made by human hands,

She Herself walks amid the heavenly choir.

JOAN: Have you come here to punish your poor creature?

Destroy me, kill me, take the thunderbolts

and let them fall upon my guilty head.

I broke my vow: I desecrated it.

I have blasphemed against your holy name.

DUNOIS: Alas! What is all this unhappy talk?

LA HIRE: (*In astonishment, to DU CHATEL.*)

Can you explain what all this is about?

DU CHATEL: I see what I see. I've been afraid of this

for some time now.

DUNOIS: What did you say?

DU CHATEL: I dare
    not tell you what I think. I wish to God
    all this was over, and the King was crowned!
LA HIRE: What? Has the terror that this flag inspired
    turned itself back to work its power on you?
    Leave the poor English to quake at this sign.
    To France's enemies it may mean fear,
    but to her loyal subjects it brings hope.
JOAN: Yes. You are right. To friends it is a sign
    of grace, to enemies a cause of terror.
    (*The coronation march is heard.*)
DUNOIS: Pick up the flag, then. Pick it up. They have
    begun the march. We must not lose a moment.
    (*They force her to take the flag. She takes it with extreme
    reluctance and leaves. The rest follow.*)

Scene 2

*The scene changes to a square in front of the cathedral. The back
of the stage is filled with SPECTATORS. From among them step
BERTRAND, CLAUDE-MARIE and ETIENNE, with MARGOT
and LOUISON after them. The coronation march is heard approaching
in the distance.*

BERTRAND:
    Listen! The music! That's them now. They're coming!
    What's the best thing to do? To get up on
    the platforms, or to press on through the crowd,
    to get a proper sight of the procession?
ETIENNE: We'll never get through that. The streets are solid
    with folk on horseback, or in carts. Why don't
    we step aside just over by these houses,
    and we'll be able to see it all quite well
    as it goes past.
CLAUDE-MARIE: It looks as if half France
    was here! The flood's so overwhelming that
    it even carried us away, and washed
    us up here, all that distance from Lorraine!

BERTRAND: Who could sit quiet in his corner, when
such great events are taking place in France?
God knows, it cost us blood and sweat enough
to get the crown put on the proper head!
And our King, who is the true and lawful one,
the one we're crowning now, he should not have
a worse attendance than the one in Paris,
him as they crowned at Saint Denis. The man
who stays away today and does not shout
'Long live the King!' is not a proper Frenchman.
(*They are joined by MARGOT and LOUISON.*)
LOUISON: Margot! we're going to see our sister, Joan!
My heart's beating so hard.
MARGOT: In all her glory,
that's how we'll see her, and we'll say: 'That's Joan!
That is our sister!'
LOUISON: I just can't believe
till I see with my own eyes, that this great person
they call the Maid of Orléans, is our Joan,
our real sister, that we lost so suddenly.
(*The march comes nearer and nearer.*)
MARGOT: You still got doubts? You'll see with your own eyes.
BERTRAND: Look! Here they come!
(*The procession is headed by flute and oboe players. They are
followed by children, dressed in white, with branches in their hands,
and behind them come two heralds. Then comes a procession of
halberdiers, followed by magistrates in their robes. Next come two
marshals with their staves, the Duke of BURGUNDY carrying
the sword of state, DUNOIS with the sceptre, other nobles carry
the crown, the orb, the staff of justice, still others bear sacrificial
offerings; after these come knights in the ceremonial dress of their
orders, choristers with censers, then two bishops, carrying the sacred
ampulla. The ARCHBISHOP carries the crucifix; JOAN follows him
with the flag. She walks with her head bowed, with uncertain step.
As they see her, her SISTERS show signs of astonishment and joy.
Behind her comes the KING, under a canopy borne by four barons,
courtiers come after them, and soldiers bring up the rear. When the
procession has passed into the cathedral, the march music stops.*)

MARGOT: Well, did you see her?

CLAUDE-MARIE: In all that golden armour.
   Walking with the banner before the King!

MARGOT: Yes, that was her. That was our sister, Joan!

LOUISON: She didn't recognise us, though. She couldn't tell
   how close her loving sisters were to her.
   She just looked at the ground, and seemed so pale,
   and she was trembling under that flag she carried –
   I can't say I liked seeing her like that.

MARGOT: Well then – I've seen our sister now, in all
   her pride and glory. Who would ever have dreamt,
   when she was herding sheep up on our mountains,
   that we would ever see her look so splendid!

LOUISON: The dream of Father's has come true, that we
   should come to Rheims, and bow down to our sister.
   That is the church that Father saw in his dream,
   and everything else he saw has happened now.
   But Father saw some sad things, bad things too…
   it makes me scared to see her grown so great!

BERTRAND: What are we doing, standing round here idle?
   Come to the church to see the ceremony.

MARGOT: Yes, come. We'll maybe meet our sister there.

LOUISON: We've seen her now: let's go back to the village.

MARGOT: What? Before we've met and talked to her?

LOUISON: She's not ours any more: her place is now
   with kings and princes – who are we to force
   ourselves on her now, out of vanity?
   She was a stranger to us, even when
   she lived with us.

MARGOT: You mean she'd feel ashamed
   of us, despise us?

BERTRAND: But the King himself
   is not ashamed of us, he had a friendly
   greeting for everyone, even the humblest.
   However high she may have climbed, she still
   is lower than the King!
   (*Trumpets and kettledrums sound inside the cathedral.*)
                    Come on inside!

(They hurry upstage, where they lose themselves in the crowd. Enter THIBAUT, dressed in black, followed by RAIMOND who is trying to restrain him.)

RAIMOND: Stop, Father Thibaut, stay out of the crowd!
 You'll only see a lot of happy faces,
 and your unhappiness will only spoil things.
 Come on, let's leave the city now, at once.

THIBAUT: Did you see my poor unfortunate girl?
 Did you get a proper look at her?

RAIMOND: Oh, please,
 come away now!

THIBAUT: You noticed how unsteady
 she walked, how pale and anxious her face looked?
 The wretched girl's aware of her position:
 this is the golden opportunity
 to save my child, and I intend to seize it.
 (He starts to go.)

RAIMOND: Stop! What are you going to do?

THIBAUT: Surprise her,
 cast her down from her vain happiness,
 and lead her back, by force if need be, to
 the God she has denied.

RAIMOND: Think what you're doing!
 Do not destroy the very thing you cherish.

THIBAUT: If her soul lives, then let her body perish!
 (JOAN comes bursting out of the cathedral, without her flag. The crowd presses up to her, adoring her and kissing her clothes; she is delayed in the background by the mob.)
 There she is now! She bursts out of the church!
 It's fear that drives her from the holy place!
 It is God's judgement which proclaims itself
 to her!

RAIMOND: Goodbye! Don't ask me to stay longer!
 I came here full of hope, and leave here full
 of sorrow. Once again I've seen your daughter,
 and feel as if I'd lost her once again.
 (He goes out. THIBAUT retires to the opposite side of the stage. JOAN disengages herself from the crowd, and comes forward.)

JOAN: I couldn't stay in there – spirits pursue me,
    the organ sounds like thunderclaps to me,
    the roof of the cathedral seems about
    to fall in on me – I must have fresh air.
    I left the banner in the sanctuary,
    I'll never, never touch the thing again!
    I felt as if I'd seen my two dear sisters,
    Margot and Louison, go floating past me,
    just like in a dream. Oh! it was only
    an apparition, they are far away,
    far, far away and quite unreachable –
    just like my childhood and my innocence.
MARGOT: (*Coming forward.*)
    It is! It's really Joan!
LOUISON: (*Hurrying up to her.*)
                    Oh, sister, sister!
JOAN: It was not madness then! It is you! Let
    me embrace you both – Louison, and Margot!
    Here in the strangeness of the lonely crowd,
    let me hug my dear sisters to my heart!
MARGOT: She does know us! You're still our sister, then!
JOAN: And your love brought you all this way to see me!
    So far, so far! Are you still angry with me,
    for leaving you like that, with no goodbyes?
LOUISON: It was God's secret mission took you away.
MARGOT: Now you are famous, and the whole world talks
    about you, you're a household word, the news
    even got as far as our quiet village
    and roused us to come and see the celebrations.
    We came to see you have your triumph. And
    we're not alone.
JOAN: Father! Father is with you!
    Where, where is he? What is he hiding for?
MARGOT: No, Father's not with us.
JOAN: He's not? He doesn't
    want to see his child? You haven't brought
    a blessing from him?

LOUISON: No, he doesn't know
    we're here.
JOAN: He doesn't know? Why doesn't he?
    You're looking all confused, and saying nothing,
    and looking at the ground. Where is my father?
MARGOT: Since you've been gone…
LOUISON: (*Gestures to her.*)   Margot!
MARGOT: Father's become
    morose…
JOAN: Morose!
LOUISON: Don't worry, though: you know
    how Father is, with all his premonitions!
    He will recover, and take heart again,
    once we have told him of your happiness.
MARGOT: So – are you happy? Yes, you must be,
    now you've got so great and honoured.
JOAN: Yes, I am –
    happy to see you, and to hear your voices
    I love so much, which take me back again
    to Father's meadows. When I drove the flocks
    out on the uplands, I was happy then,
    I might have been in Paradise: is there
    no way I can be so – become so once again!
    (*She hides her face on LOUISON's breast. CLAUDE-MARIE,
    ETIENNE and BERTRAND appear and remain standing
    timidly some distance away.*)
MARGOT: Etienne! Bertrand! Claude- Marie! Come here!
    Our sister is not proud: she is more gentle
    and speaks more kindly than she ever did
    when she was living with us in the village.
    (*The others come closer, and start to hold out their hands to her.
    JOAN stares at them fixedly, in a state of astonishment.*)
JOAN: Where have I been? No, tell me! Was it all
    a long, long dream, and now am I awake?
    Have I left Domremy? It isn't true.
    I fell asleep under the magic tree,
    and now I've woken up, and you are all
    around me, all the people I am used to!

I only dreamt about those kings and battles
and wars, they were just shadows passing by me,
one's dreams can be so clear under that tree.
How would you get to Rheims? Or how would I?
I never left Domremy, never, never!
Confess it now, and make my heart much happier.

LOUISON: We are in Rheims. It wasn't just a dream.
You really did those things – collect yourself,
and look around you. Feel that shining armour.

(*JOAN puts her hand to her breast, comes to herself and shudders.*)

BERTRAND: I was the one you had the helmet from.

CLAUDE-MARIE:
It is no wonder that you think you're dreaming:
the things you have achieved could hardly be
more wonderful if you had have dreamt them.

JOAN: (*Quickly.*)   Come!
Let us run away, I will come back with you;
back to the village, back to Father's arms.

LOUISON: Oh yes, come with us!

JOAN: All these people want
to raise me far above where I belong.
You knew me when I was a little child;
you love me, but you do not worship me.

MARGOT: Could you give up all this magnificence?

JOAN: I'd throw it all away, I hate the pomp
that separates my heart from all of yours.
I want to be a shepherdess again.
And I will serve you like the lowest servant,
atone with the strongest penance that there is,
for having vainly raised myself above you.

(*Trumpets sound. Enter from the cathedral CHARLES, in full coronation regalia, Agnès SOREL, the ARCHBISHOP, the Duke of BURGUNDY, DUNOIS, LA HIRE, DU CHATEL, with knights, courtiers and people. As the KING comes forward, everyone shouts repeatedly: 'Long live the King! Long live King Charles the Seventh!' Trumpets strike up. At a signal given by the KING, the HERALDS raise their staffs to command silence.*)

CHARLES:

> Frenchmen! and friends! We thank you for your loves!
> The crown, that God has placed upon our head,
> was conquered by the sword, and it is wet
> with the noble blood of citizens of France.
> But may the olive branch now grow in peace
> about it. Thanks to all who fought for us!
> And for all those who fought against us, let
> there be an amnesty; since God has shown
> us mercy, let our first word as King be – mercy!

ALL: Long live the King! God save King Charles the Good!

CHARLES: From God alone, the highest King of all,

> we do derive the crown of France's kings,
> but we receive it from His hand in form
> both manifest and visible.
>
> (*He turns to JOAN.*)
>
> Here stands the one whom Heaven sent to give
> you back your true, hereditary King,
> and break the chains of foreign tyranny.
> Her name shall stand beside that of Saint Denis,
> protector of our land, and to her glory
> an altar shall be raised.

ALL: Hail to the Maid!

> Hail to the Saviour!
>
> (*Trumpets.*)

CHARLES: (*To JOAN.*)

> If you are sprung from mortal stock, as we are,
> tell us what we can do to give you pleasure;
> but if your native country is in Heaven,
> if in that virgin body you enclose
> the radiance of a nature that's divine,
> then take the blindfold from our muddied senses,
> and let yourself be seen in all the brilliance
> that Heaven sees you in, so that we may
> adore you in the dust.
>
> (*A general silence; all eyes are turned on her.*)

111

JOAN: (*With a sudden cry.*) Oh God! My father!
　　(*THIBAUT steps out of the crowd and stands directly opposite her.*)
SEVERAL VOICES: Her father!
THIBAUT: 　　　　　　　　　Yes, her miserable father,
　　the father of this wretched girl, set on
　　by God's command to accuse her, my own child.
BURGUNDY: What was that?
DU CHATEL: 　　　　　　Terrible things will come to light now.
THIBAUT: (*To the King.*)
　　You think you have been saved by the power of God?
　　You are betrayed, Prince! Frenchmen, you are blinded!
　　You have been saved, but by the powers of Hell!
　　(*All recoil in horror.*)
DUNOIS: Is the fellow mad?
THIBAUT: 　　　　　　　　No, he is not, but you are,
　　and all these people here, and this wise bishop,
　　all who believe God would reveal himself
　　in the person of a slattern scullery-maid.
　　See if she dares, before her father's face,
　　assert the cheating, juggling lie with which
　　she has deceived her King and the whole nation.
　　Answer me, in the name of God the Father,
　　Son and Holy Ghost, do you belong
　　among the ranks of the pure and innocent?
　　(*A general silence. All eyes are fixed on her. She stands motionless.*)
SOREL: God! She says nothing.
THIBAUT: 　　　　　　　　No more she dare, in face
　　of that dread name, feared in the pit of Hell
　　itself! What? Her a saint, and sent by God!
　　It was dreamed up in an unholy place,
　　under a magic tree, where evil spirits
　　have kept their Sabbath from time immemorial.
　　That's where she bartered her immortal soul
　　to the enemy of Mankind, if he would give her
　　the glory of some passing earthly fame.

Have her roll back her sleeve, look at the marks
Hell put on her to know her as his own!

BURGUNDY: This is appalling! But one must believe
a father who denounces his own child!

DUNOIS: No, we do not have to believe a madman
who brings shame on himself by such an charge.

SOREL: (*To JOAN.*) Just speak, and break this miserable silence!
We all believe in you – we trust in you
implicitly. One word, one single word,
spoken by you will be enough for us –
but speak! destroy this dreadful calumny.
Say you are innocent, and we will believe you.
(*JOAN stands without moving. SOREL retreats from her in
horror.*)

LA HIRE: The girl is frightened. Horror and surprise
have stopped her tongue. Innocence itself
would be struck dumb by so obscene a charge.
(*He approaches her.*)
Joan, pull yourself together. Innocence
has a language of its own, a look of power
which blasts the slanderer like a lightning flash:
Rise up in righteous anger, raise your eyes,
and shame and punish the unworthy doubts
that have been cast upon your holy virtue.
(*JOAN stands without moving. LA HIRE draws back, horrified.
The general commotion increases.*)

DUNOIS: Why is the crowd afraid? The princes, even?
She is innocent! I pledge my honour as
a prince for her. There I throw down my gauntlet:
will anyone here now dare call her guilty?
(*There is a violent clap of thunder; all stand petrified.*)

THIBAUT: In the name of God who thunders, answer me!
Say you are guiltless, and deny that Satan
is in your heart: prove that I am a liar.
(*A second, louder thunderclap; the crowd flees in all directions.*)

BURGUNDY: Heaven preserve us! These are fearful omens.

DU CHATEL: Come! Come, Your Majesty! Let's leave this place.

ARCHBISHOP: (*To JOAN.*)

In the name of God I ask you: are you silent
out of a sense of innocence, or guilt?
If it is for you the thunder speaks
then take hold of the cross and give a sign.
(*JOAN stands without moving. Renewed, violent claps of thunder. King CHARLES, SOREL, the ARCHBISHOP, BURGUNDY, LA HIRE and DU CHATEL leave.*)

DUNOIS: You are my bride – I have believed in you
since we first met, and I believe you still.
I trust you more than all these indications,
more than the thunder even, rolling up there.
Your silence springs out of your righteous anger;
wrapped in the knowledge of your innocence, you
disdain to contradict such foul suspicions.
Disdain it then, but trust yourself to me,
who never had a doubt that you were innocent.
Say nothing, not a word: just give me your hand,
in sign and token that your trust is firm
in my strong arm and in your own good cause.
(*He holds out his hand to her; she turns away from him with a convulsive movement. He stands fixed to the spot with horror. DU CHATEL re-enters.*)

DU CHATEL: Joan of Arc! The King gives his permission
for you to leave the city unmolested.
The gates are open for you. There is no
need to fear harm. The King's peace will protect you.
You are to follow me, Count Dunois. There is
no honour to be gained by staying here.
What an ending!
(*He leaves. DUNOIS recovers from his stupefaction, casts a last look at JOAN and goes out. She is quite alone for a while. RAIMOND appears, and remains standing at a distance for a while, looking at her in silent agony. Then he goes up to her and takes her by the hand.*)

RAIMOND: This is our opportunity. Take it! Come!
The streets are empty now. Give me your hand.
I will show you the way.

(On seeing him, she shows her first sign of feeling, staring fixedly at him, and raising her eyes to Heaven. Then she seizes him violently by the hand and goes out.)

End of Act Four.

ACT FIVE

Scene 1

A wild forest. Charcoal burners' huts in the distance. It is completely dark; violent thunder and lightning and, intermittently, the sound of gunfire. A CHARCOAL BURNER and his WIFE enter.

CHARCOAL BURNER:
> This is a cruel and a murderous storm.
> The heavens threaten to pour down on us
> in streams of fire, the daytime is so dark,
> that you can see the very stars at noon.
> The storm is raging like all Hell let loose;
> the ground shakes, and the ancient ash trees creak
> and bend their ruined tops. This dreadful warfare
> above our heads, that teaches gentleness
> even to savage beasts, so that they tamely
> cower in their lairs, can bring no peace to men.
> Mixed with the howling of the wind and storm
> you can still hear the roar and crack of gunfire.
> Both armies are so close to one another
> that nothing but the forest separates them,
> and any moment things could end in blood.

CHARCOAL BURNER'S WIFE:
> Heaven protect us! But the enemy
> were beaten hollow and scattered, weren't they now?
> How can they come to frighten us again?

CHARCOAL BURNER:
> That's because they no longer fear the King,
> ever since the Maid was found to be
> a witch, in Rheims, the Evil One won't fight for
> us no more, and everything has gone
> astray.

CHARCOAL BURNER'S WIFE:
> Listen! There's someone there. Who is it?

(Enter RAIMOND and JOAN.)

RAIMOND: I can see huts. Come on, we can find shelter

here from this terrible storm. You cannot stand
this any longer; it is three days now
you have been wandering about, avoiding
the sight of human beings, and you have
had nothing to eat but wild roots you've dug up.
(*The storm subsides; it grows bright and clear.*)
These are kind-hearted people, charcoal burners.
Let us go in.

CHARCOAL BURNER: You look in need of rest.
Come in, and welcome to what our poor roof
can offer.

CHARCOAL BURNER'S WIFE:
What would a young girl want with weapons?
Well, to be sure, now, these are troubled times
when even women have to put on armour!
They say the Queen herself, that Isabeau,
is seen in arms around the enemy camp,
and there's a girl, a shepherd's lass, they say,
has been in battle for our lord the King.

CHARCOAL BURNER:
What are you saying? Get back in the hut,
get the girl something to revive her.
(*The CHARCOAL BURNER's WIFE goes into the hut.*)

RAIMOND: (*To JOAN.*) You see,
not everybody in the world is cruel,
there are kind hearts, even in the wilderness.
Be cheerful then! The storm has spent itself,
the sun is going down, and all is peace.

CHARCOAL BURNER:
I suppose you will be wanting to join up
with the King's army, seeing you're under arms.
Be careful! the English camp is just near here;
and their patrols comb the forest all the time.

RAIMOND: How can we avoid them?

CHARCOAL BURNER: Just stay here
until our lad gets back from town, and he
can take you down a secret way where you
will have no need to fear. We know the woods.

RAIMOND: (*To JOAN.*)

Take your helmet, and your armour off.

They only give you away – and won't protect you.

(*JOAN shakes her head.*)

CHARCOAL BURNER:

The girl looks very sad – quiet! Who's coming?

(*The CHARCOAL BURNER's WIFE comes out of the hut with a cup. Enter the CHARCOAL BURNER's SON.*)

CHARCOAL BURNER'S WIFE:

It's just the boy, as we expected back.

(*To JOAN.*) Drink up now, gentle miss. God's blessing with it!

CHARCOAL BURNER: (*To SON.*)

Are you back then, son? What news?

(*The CHARCOAL BURNER's SON has fixed his eyes on JOAN, who is just lifting the cup to her lips. He recognises her, goes up to her, and snatches the cup away from her mouth.*)

CHARCOAL BURNER'S SON: Mother! Mother!

What are you doing? Who have you taken in?

That is the witch of Orléans!

CHARCOAL BURNER and his WIFE: God have mercy!

(*They cross themselves and run away.*)

JOAN: (*Calmly and quietly.*)

You see, the curse pursues me. They all run

away from me: now take care of yourself

and leave me too.

RAIMOND: Me leave you? Now? And who

will be with you?

JOAN: I shall not want for company.

You heard the thunder up above my head.

It is my fate that leads me. Do not worry;

I will reach my goal without my having to seek it.

RAIMOND: Where will you go ? On one side are the English,

who have sworn to have a cruel and bloody vengeance:

on the other, our people, who have cast you out…

JOAN: Nothing will happen to me, except what must.

RAIMOND: Who will find food for you? Who will protect you

from savage beasts and still more savage men?

Who will look after you if you get sick?

JOAN: I know all about herbs and roots. My sheep
  taught me to tell the poisonous from the healthy.
  I understand the sky at night and I
  can read the weather in the clouds, and hear
  the murmuring of springs deep underground.
  People do not need much, and Nature is
  so rich in everything.

RAIMOND: (*Takes her hand.*) Won't you search your heart?
  And make your peace with God – come back into
  the bosom of the Church in penitence?

JOAN: You too, you think I'm guilty of that sin?

RAIMOND: How could I not? Your silence was confession…

JOAN: You followed me into poverty and exile,
  you were the only one who has been faithful,
  who bound himself to me, when all the world
  had cast me off: you too think I'm an outcast,
  who has renounced her God –
  (*RAIMOND says nothing.*)   Oh, that is hard!

RAIMOND: (*In astonishment.*)
  You mean you really aren't a witch?

JOAN: A witch!

RAIMOND: And all those miracles, you really did perform them
  by the power of God and all his saints?

JOAN: How else?

RAIMOND:
  But when they brought that hideous charge against you,
  you said nothing! – Now you speak, but then,
  before the King, when it was so important
  to speak out, you said nothing. Not a word.

JOAN: I submitted in silence to the destiny
  that God, my master, has ordained for me.

RAIMOND: But how could you say nothing to your father?

JOAN: Because it came from him, it came from God,
  and correction will come as from a father's hand.

RAIMOND: But even the heavens seemed to speak against you.

JOAN: If Heaven spoke, that was why I did not.

RAIMOND: With a single word you could have cleared yourself,
  instead you let the world believe this error.

JOAN: It was no error, it was destiny.

RAIMOND: You suffered all this shame in innocence,
　　without one word of protest from your lips?
　　I'm just amazed at you, I'm really shaken,
　　and feel relief from the bottom of my heart!
　　I am so ready and happy to believe you.
　　It was so hard for me to think you guilty,
　　but I could not believe that any one
　　would bear so terrible a charge in silence.

JOAN: Could I deserve to be God's messenger
　　and not give blind obedience to His will?
　　Nor am I quite as wretched as you think.
　　I suffer want, but that is no disaster
　　for one of my rank: I'm exiled, an outcast,
　　but in the wilderness I have learned to know
　　myself. It was when the glare of honours shone
　　about me that my heart was in such conflict.
　　When I seemed most to be envied in the world,
　　that was the time when I was most unhappy.
　　Now I am cured, and this great storm in Nature,
　　that threatened an end to all things, is my friend.
　　It has cleansed the world, and me: peace is within me.
　　Come what will, I feel no further weakness.

RAIMOND: Come with me, now, let's hurry to make known
　　your spotless innocence to all the world!

JOAN: He who sent this confusion will dissolve it,
　　The fruit of Destiny falls when it is ripe!
　　A day will come to vindicate me, when
　　all those who cast me out and slandered me
　　will be aware of what they did in madness,
　　and then the tears will flow for my sad fate.

RAIMOND: Am I to wait in silence, then, till Chance…

JOAN: (*Gently taking his hand.*)
　　All you can see of things is what you see:
　　your sight is still made dim by bonds of earth.
　　I have seen immortality face to face.
　　God marks the fall of every hair from every head.
　　Look, over there, the sun is going down.

As sure as it will rise again tomorrow,

the day of Truth will just as surely dawn.

(*In the distance, Queen ISABEAU appears with SOLDIERS.*)

ISABEAU: (*Still offstage.*)

This is the way into the English camp!

RAIMOND: The enemy! We're lost!

(*SOLDIERS enter, notice JOAN and reel back in terror.*)

ISABEAU: Why have you halted?

SOLDIERS: Heaven preserve us!

ISABEAU: Frightened of a ghost?

Call yourselves soldiers? Cowards is what you are!

What?

(*She pushes through the ranks, to the front, and starts back as she sees the MAID.*)

                  What do I see? What have we here? Surrender!

You are my prisoner.

JOAN: Yes.

(*RAIMOND flees with signs of despair.*)

ISABEAU: Clap her in irons!

(*The SOLDIERS advance timidly on JOAN, who holds out her arms to be chained.*)

Is this the fearsome dreaded creature, then?

The one who scattered all our troops like sheep?

And now she cannot defend even herself!

Can she do miracles only for her believers,

and turns into a woman when she meets

a man? Why have you left your army? Where

is Count Dunois, your knight and your protector?

JOAN: I have been banished.

ISABEAU: What? You have been banished?

The Dauphin had you banished?

JOAN: Do not ask.

I am in your hands – do with me as you please.

ISABEAU: Banished, for having saved him from the pit!

For putting the crown upon his head at Rheims!

For making him King over the whole of France!

Banished! Now there I recognise my son!

Take her into the camp, and show the army

the fearful ghost they were so frightened of!
That thing a sorceress? All the magic is
madness and cowardice in your own hearts.
She is a *fool*, who sacrificed herself
for a king, and now receives a king's reward
for what she did – take her to Lionel –
I send him France's fortunes in a parcel,
I shall be there at once.

JOAN: To Lionel! Kill me
here on the spot, but do not send me there!

ISABEAU: (*To the SOLDIERS.*)
You have your orders! Obey them! Off with her!
(*She leaves.*)

JOAN: Englishmen, do not let me escape alive
out of your hands. You must have your revenge!
Take out your swords and plunge them in my heart,
then drag my lifeless body to the feet
of your commanding officer. Remember,
I was the one who killed your bravest men,
who had no pity for any one of you,
who shed whole rivers of English blood, who took
away from all those brave, heroic English boys,
the happy day when they could go back home!
Now take your bloody vengeance! Kill me now
now that you have me; you may not always see me
as weak as this…

OFFICER: You heard the Queen. Do as she says.

JOAN: Must I
be made more wretched even than before?
Holy and terrible one, hard is your hand.
Am I cast out for ever from your grace?
No angel comes, and miracles have an end:
Heaven's gates are shut; God turns away His face.
(*She follows the SOLDIERS out.*)

Scene 2

The French camp. DUNOIS between the ARCHBISHOP and DU CHATEL.

ARCHBISHOP: Prince, you must overcome this black depression.
    Come with us. Come back to the King! Do not
    desert the common cause at such a moment,
    when new emergencies need your strong arm.

DUNOIS: Why are there new emergencies? Why is
    the enemy back again? All had been done:
    France was victorious and the war was over.
    The one who saved us you sent into exile:
    now save yourselves! I have no wish to see
    the camp again, where she no longer is.

DU CHATEL: Prince, be better advised, and do not leave us
    with such an answer.

DUNOIS: Du Chatel, be silent!
    I have no wish to hear from you, I hate you.
    You were the first to doubt her.

ARCHBISHOP: Which of us
    did not doubt her, and who would not have wavered
    on that unhappy day, when all the signs
    spoke so against her! We were shocked and stunned:
    the blow had struck too deeply to our hearts.
    At such a terrible moment who could remain
    objective? But our better judgement is
    restored to us; we see her as she lived
    among us, and we find no fault with her.
    We are confused: we fear we may have done
    a terrible wrong – the King repents, the Duke
    blames himself, La Hire is desperate,
    and every heart is plunged in deepest grief.

DUNOIS: She lie to us? If truth should ever be
    made visible, it would have to wear her features.
    If there is innocence, fidelity,
    and purity of heart on earth, then they
    must dwell on her lips, and in her clear-set eyes!

ARCHBISHOP: If Heaven would only intervene and send
    some sign, some miracle that could explain
    this mystery hidden to our mortal sight.
    But in whatever way it is explained,
    one way or other, we are guilty men:
    either by using the Devil's arts to fight
    our wars with, or by banishing a saint!
    In either case, the wrath of God will be
    called down upon our most unhappy country!
    (*Enter a NOBLEMAN.*)
NOBLEMAN: There is a shepherd, asking for Your Highness.
    He wants to speak with you most urgently.
    He comes, or so he says, from the Maid…
DUNOIS: Quickly!
    Bring him in! He comes from her!
    (*The NOBLEMAN opens the doors to admit RAIMOND.*
    DUNOIS hurries over to him.)   Where is she?
    Where is the Maid?
RAIMOND: Hail, noble Prince! I am
    most blest to see this pious bishop with you,
    this holy man, protector of the oppressed,
    and father of the lost.
DUNOIS: Where is the Maid!
ARCHBISHOP: Tell us, my son.
RAIMOND: My lord, she is not a witch!
    By God and all His saints, I swear she's not!
    The people are mistaken. You have banished
    the innocent, cast out one sent by God!
DUNOIS: Where is she? Tell us!
RAIMOND: I was with her when
    she took flight through the forest of the Ardennes,
    where she revealed her inmost heart to me.
    May I die under torture, may my soul
    forfeit its share of everlasting bliss,
    my Lord, if she is not free of all sin!
DUNOIS: The sun in Heaven itself is not more pure!
    Where is she? Tell us!

RAIMOND: Oh, if God has turned
    your hearts, then hurry, rescue her – she is
    a prisoner of the English.
DUNOIS: A prisoner!
ARCHBISHOP: Oh, poor unhappy girl!
RAIMOND: In the Ardennes
    while we were seeking shelter, she was taken
    by the Queen, who sent her over to the English.
    Oh, save her, as she once saved all of you,
    from a dreadful death!
DUNOIS: To arms, then! Sound the alarm!
    Summon the army to battle! Let all France
    arm herself! Our honour is in pawn.
    The crown, France's safeguard's stolen, gone.
    Set all your bloods, your lives upon the cast!
    She must be freed before this day is done!
    (*Exeunt.*)

Scene 3

A watchtower, with an opening above.

FASTOLF: (*Entering in haste.*)
    The people can no longer be held back.
    They scream at us to put the Maid to death.
    Resistance would be pointless. Kill her now,
    and throw her head down off the battlements.
    Only her blood will pacify the troops.
ISABEAU: (*Entering.*)
    They are using scaling ladders to mount the attack!
    Do what the people ask, or would you wait
    until in their blind rage they overturn
    the tower and kill us all along with it?
LIONEL: Let them attack! As fiercely as they like!
    The walls are strong, and I shall find my grave
    under its ruins, sooner than be forced
    to do their bidding. Joan, now answer me!
    Marry me, and I will shield you from the world.
ISABEAU: Are you a man?

LIONEL: Your own have cast you out.
    You are now free from further obligations
    to your unworthy fatherland. The cowards
    who sought your hand have all abandoned you,
    not daring to do battle for your honour.
    But I shall stand by you against my people
    and against yours. You once let me believe
    my life was of some value to you. Then
    I was your enemy, now your only friend!
JOAN: You are the hated enemy both of me
    and of my people. Common ground cannot
    exist between the two of us. Love you
    I cannot, but if your heart feels for me,
    then let it work a blessing for our nations.
    Draw off your armies from our territories,
    give back the keys of all the cities you
    have taken, and make restitution of
    all you have robbed, free all your prisoners,
    send hostages to guarantee the treaty,
    and I will offer peace in my King's name.
ISABEAU: You are dictating terms to us, in fetters?
JOAN: And do it soon, since do it you will have to.
    France will not submit to English chains.
    No, that will never happen, never! She
    would sooner be a grave for all your armies.
    Your best are dead: think of a safe withdrawal.
    Your fame is lost, your power lies in ruins.
ISABEAU: The girl is mad. How can you listen to her?
    (*A CAPTAIN hurries in.*)
CAPTAIN: General, you must put the men up in battle order;
    the French are coming on with standards raised;
    their weapons shine and glitter through the valley.
JOAN: (*As if inspired.*)
    The French are coming on! Now, you proud English,
    into the field with you! It's time to fight!
FASTOLF: Madwoman, I should moderate your joy:
    you will not live as long as this day's end.

JOAN: My people will have victory: I shall die.

    Those brave men will not need me any more.

LIONEL: Weaklings! I scorn them! We have chased them off

    a score of times in terror from the field,

    before this heroine fought for them, I feel

    nothing but contempt for their whole nation,

    except for one, and her they sent to exile!

    Fastolf, come! we shall give them such a day,

    as they've not seen since Poitiers or Crécy!

    You, Madame, will remain here in the tower,

    and guard her, till the battle is decided.

    I leave you fifty men for your protection.

FASTOLF: What! Are we going out to meet the enemy,

    leaving this maniac behind our backs?

JOAN: Are you so frightened of a girl in chains?

LIONEL: Give me your word, Joan, you will not escape.

JOAN: The only thing I want is to escape.

ISABEAU: Put triple fetters on her. I'll engage

    my life on it, she shall not get away.

    (*JOAN is fettered, with heavy chains around her arms and legs.*)

LIONEL: (*To JOAN.*) You wanted it like this. You forced us to it.

    It's still your choice. Renounce France, and embrace

    the English flag. You will be free: these madmen

    who now scream for your blood, will be your slaves.

FASTOLF: (*Urgently.*) General, we must go now.

JOAN: Save your breath.

    The French are coming on – defend yourselves!

    (*Trumpets sound. LIONEL hurries out.*)

FASTOLF: Madame, you understand what you must do!

    If the day should go against us, and you see

    our armies in retreat…

ISABEAU: (*Drawing a dagger.*) You need not fear.

    She will not live to see us in defeat.

FASTOLF: (*To JOAN.*)

    You know what to expect. *Now* pray, if you can,

    success attend the arms of France!

    (*He goes out.*)

JOAN: I shall!
   That no one can prevent me doing. Listen!
   The war-march of my people! How it echoes
   deep in my heart, foretelling victory!
   Ruin to England! Victory to France!
   Come on, my brave, brave men: the Maid is near you,
   she cannot bear the flag ahead of you
   as she did once – she is bound in heavy fetters.
   But from her prison walls, her soul swings free,
   borne on the wings of your brave songs of war.
ISABEAU: (*To a SOLDIER.*)
   Get up into the watch-tower that overlooks
   the battlefield, and tell us what is happening.
   (*The SOLDIER goes up.*)
JOAN: Be brave, my people! This fight is your last!
   One final victory and they will surrender.
ISABEAU: What can you see?
SOLDIER: They are already fighting.
   A wild knight in a tiger skin has darted
   out of the ranks, leading his cavalry.
JOAN: Dunois! Come on, come on, brave soldier, fight!
   Victory is on your side!
SOLDIER: The Duke
   of Burgundy is making for the bridge.
ISABEAU: I'd like to see a dozen lances run
   his false heart through, the traitor that he is!
SOLDIER: Lord Fastolf's putting up a strong resistance.
   They have dismounted now; they're fighting hand
   to hand, the Duke's men and our own.
ISABEAU: But can't
   you see the Dauphin? Don't you recognise
   the royal insignia?
SOLDIER: Everything is covered
   in dust. I cannot make out anything.
JOAN: If he had my eyes, or if I was up
   where he is, not a detail would escape me.
   I can count birds in flight, I can pick out
   the falcon hovering miles up in the sky.

SOLDIER: Down by the trench there is a dreadful scrimmage.
    That's where the greatest nobles seem to be.
ISABEAU: But is our flag still flying?
SOLDIER: High in the air.
JOAN: If I could just see through the cracks in the walls,
    I would control the battle with my eyes.
SOLDIER: Oh, God! What do I see! The general
    has been surrounded.
ISABEAU: (*Drawing the dagger on JOAN.*)
                        Die, witch!
SOLDIER: (*Quickly.*)   No, they freed him.
    Now the brave Fastolf is attacking from
    the rear – he breaks into their thickest ranks.
ISABEAU: (*Putting up the dagger again.*)
    Your angel spoke.
SOLDIER: Look! Look! They're running away!
ISABEAU: Who are?
SOLDIER: The French and the Burgundians.
    The field is covered with the fugitives.
JOAN: My God! My God! Thou wilt not thus forsake me?
SOLDIER: They're leading off a badly-wounded man.
    A lot of men are running to his aid.
    It is a prince.
ISABEAU: One of the French, or ours?
SOLDIER: They're taking off his helmet. Count Dunois!
JOAN: (*Grasping her chains convulsively.*)
    And I am nothing but a girl in chains!
SOLDIER:
    Wait! Look! Who's that in the blue cloak fringed with gold?
JOAN: (*With animation.*)
    The King!
SOLDIER: His horse is shy – it rears – it plunges –
    he makes his way to the front with difficulty.
    (*JOAN accompanies his words with passionate reactions.*)
    Our men are moving up now at the gallop –
    they've caught up with him – they've got him surrounded!
JOAN: Oh God, have you no angels left in Heaven!

ISABEAU: (*With mocking laughter.*)

Now is your moment! Saviour, save them now!

JOAN: (*Falling on her knees, and praying in a voice of intense power.*) Hear me, O God, in my hour of most need!

To you in Heaven I send my soul in prayer.

You can make cobwebs strong as great ships' cables,

to your omnipotence it is a trifle

to make these iron fetters thin as cobwebs –

if you so will, these chains will fall away,

the prison walls divide – you gave your aid

to Samson, when he was in chains, and blinded,

bearing his proud enemies' bitter scorn –

trusting in you, he grasped the pillars of

his prison, strained and brought it down in ruin!

SOLDIER: Hurrah! Hurrah!

ISABEAU: What is it now?

SOLDIER: The King

is taken prisoner.

JOAN: God be with me now!

(*She has seized her chains powerfully in both hands, and snapped them. At the same instant she falls on the SOLDIER nearest to her, snatches his sword from him, and runs out. Everyone stares after her in complete astonishment.*)

ISABEAU: (*After a long pause.*)

What was that? Did I dream it? Where did she go?

How could she snap those chains? They weighed a ton.

I would not have believed it for the world,

had I not seen it happen before my eyes.

SOLDIER: (*On the watch-tower.*)

Has she got wings? Or did a whirlwind come

and carry her away?

ISABEAU: Is she down there now?

SOLDIER: She's striding through the thickest of the fight.

She's faster than the eye can follow – now

she's here – she's there – she seems to be in twenty

places at once! She penetrates the ranks –

everything is giving way before her –

the French are standing firm: they are regrouping!

Oh, God, look there! Our men have all thrown down
their arms, the flags are being lowered –

ISABEAU: What?!

Is she cheating us of certain victory?

SOLDIER:

She's pressing on towards the King – she's reached him –
she's pulled him by main force out of the fighting –
Lord Fastolf's fallen – the general has been taken!

ISABEAU: Come down from there, I wish to hear no more.

SOLDIER: Fly, Madam, fly! The fortress is surprised.

A body of men is making for the tower.

(*He climbs down.*)

ISABEAU: (*Drawing a sword.*)

Then fight, you cowards!

(*LA HIRE enters with SOLDIERS. At his appearance the
QUEEN's SOLDIERS lay down their arms.*)

LA HIRE: (*Approaching her respectfully.*)

Your Majesty, surrender
to our superior power – your knights have all
done so – and further opposition would be useless!
Accept my services; give order where
you wish to be accompanied.

ISABEAU: Anywhere

I do not have to set eyes on the Dauphin.

(*She gives up her sword, and follows him with the SOLDIERS.*)

Scene 4

*The scene changes to the battlefield. SOLDIERS with waving banners
fill the background. In front of them are the KING and the Duke of
BURGUNDY, with JOAN lying, mortally wounded, in their arms,
showing no sign of life. They come slowly forward. Agnès SOREL
bursts in.*

SOREL: You are alive – and free – and mine again!

CHARLES: Alive and free, yes, but at what a price!

(*Pointing to JOAN.*)

SOREL: Joan! Oh, my God, she's dying!

BURGUNDY: She is dead.

See how an angel goes! Look how she lies,
in no pain, peaceful as a sleeping child.
The peace of Heaven plays about her face,
no breath is left in her, but there is still
some warmth of life remaining in her hand.

CHARLES: She's gone – she will not wake ever again.
Her eyes will never see the sights of earth.
She floats above us, a transfigured spirit,
no longer conscious of our grief or penitence.

SOREL: Her eyes are opening. She is alive!

BURGUNDY: (*Astonished.*)
Has she come back to us out of the grave?
Has she defeated Death? She's rising, standing!

JOAN: (*Stands upright, and looks about her.*)
Where am I?

BURGUNDY: With your friends, Joan, your own people.

CHARLES: In the arms of those who love you, and your King.

JOAN: (*After staring fixedly at him for some time.*)
No, I am not a sorceress. Be sure
I am not.

CHARLES: You are holy as an angel.
Our eyes were dimmed; the veil of night was on them.

JOAN: (*Looking about her with a happy smile.*)
And am I really back with my own people?
and not an outcast any more, and not despised?
They do not curse me, they look at me kindly.
Yes, now I see it all again distinctly!
That is my King! And that is France's flag!
But I don't see my flag – where has it gone?
I must not come without my flag. It was
given in trust to me by my great master:
I have to lay it down before His throne:
I can do this, since I was true to it.

CHARLES: (*His face turned away.*)
Give her the flag!
(*It is handed to her. She stands quite upright and unsupported,
with the flag in her hand. The sky is lit up with a rosy glow.*)

132

JOAN: Look! Do you see the rainbow in the sky?
   Heaven is opening its golden gates.
   She stands in glory amid the angel choir,
   her ever–living son held to her breast:
   now she holds out her arms to me, and smiles.
   What's happening to me? Clouds lift me up –
   my heavy armour's changing – I am on wings –
   I rise – up – up – earth falls away so fast –
   the pain is short, the joy is everlasting!
   (*The flag falls from her hand, and she sinks down upon it, dead.
   All stand for a long time, speechless with emotion. At a slight
   sign from the KING all the flags are lowered over her, so that
   she is completely covered by them.*)

   The End.

WILLIAM TELL

(WILHELM TELL)

A NEW YEAR'S GIFT FOR 1805

Characters

HERMANN GESSLER, *Imperial viceroy in Schwyz and Uri*
WERNER, FREIHERR VON ATTINGHAUSEN, *Banneret*
ULRICH VON RUDENZ, *his nephew*

Citizens of Schwyz:
WERNER STAUFFACHER
KONRAD HUNN
ITEL REDING
HANS AUF DER MAUER
JOERG IM HOFE
ULRICH DER SCHMIED
JOST VON WEILER

Of Uri:
WALTER FUERST
WILLIAM TELL
ROESSELMANN, *the Minister*
PETERMANN, *the Sexton*
KUONI, *the Shepherd*
WERNI, *the Huntsman*
RUODI, *the Fisherman*

Of Unterwalden:
ARNOLD VON MELCHTHAL
KONRAD BAUMGARTEN
MEIER VON SARNEN
STRUTH VON WINKELRIED
KLAUS VON DER FLUEE
BURKHARDT AM BUEHEL
ARNOLD VON SEWA

PFEIFFER OF LUCERNE

KUNZ VON GERSAU

JENNI, *Fisher boy*

SEPPI, *Shepherd boy*

GERTRUD, *Stauffacher's wife*

HEDWIG, *Tell's wife, Fuerst's daughter*

BERTA VON BRUNECK, *a rich heiress*

ARMGARD, MECHTHILD, ELSBET, HILDEGARD,
peasant women

WALTHER, WILHELM, *Tell's children*

FRIESSHARDT, LEUTHOLD, *Soldiers*

RUDOLF DER HARRAS, *Gessler's stable-master*

JOHANNES PARRICIDA, *Duke of Swabia*

STUESSI, *Fieldguard*

HERALD OF URI

IMPERIAL MESSENGER

MASTER STONEMASON, APPRENTICES, WORKMEN

PUBLIC ANNOUNCER

BROTHERS OF MERCY

HORSEMEN of Gessler and Landenberg

Many citizens, men and women from the canton towns

This translation of *William Tell* was first performed as a rehearsed reading in the Olivier Theatre on 13 October 2005, as part of the National Theatre's Schiller festival marking the bicentenary of his death. The reading was directed by Garry Cooper.

ACT ONE

Scene 1

Steep, rocky shore of the Lake of Lucerne in the canton Schwyz, near the border of nid dem Wald and Uri: a hut near the shore, and JENNI, a fisher boy, in a boat. Beyond the lake can be seen the green meadows, the villages and houses of Schwyz in the bright sunshine. To the spectators' left are the mountain peaks; to the right in the distant background one sees the glaciers. Before the curtain rises, one can hear the sound of the Alpine cowherd's tune, the 'Ranz des Vaches', and the harmonies of the cowbells, which continue for a while after the curtain goes up.

JENNI: (*Singing in his boat.*)
    The lake is so clear, the waters invite,
    The boy falls asleep on the bank, in delight,
        He hears then a ringing,
            A heavenly song,
                Like angels singing,
                    All summer long.

    And when he awakes from the dream he was in,
    The waters are lapping as high as his chin,
        A voice calls from the deep:
            'Sweet boy, you shall see
                How I charm those who sleep
                And draw them to me.'
SEPPI: (*On the mountainside.*) Green pastures, farewell,
        And you, sunlit meadows,
        The shepherd must leave you,
        The summer is gone.
    We go to the heights, nor return to the plain
    Till the cuckoo calls, till songs are heard again,
    Till flowers clothe the land as bright as day,
    Till springs have thawed, and flow again in May.
        Green pastures, farewell!
        And you, sunlit meadows!
        The shepherd must leave you,
        The summer is gone.

WERNI: (*Appearing opposite, high up on the rock.*)
Here's a storm on the heights, so much is clear,
Nothing frightens the huntsman in his career.
    He ventures boldly,
    Over icy fields.
    No spring glitters coldly –
    No crop it yields.
Beneath his feet is a misty floor;
He knows the cities of men no more.
    Through the gap in the clouds
    The world is seen,
    Deep under the waters,
    The fields of green…
(*The landscape changes, there is a hollow reverberation from the mountains, shadows of the clouds chase over the region. RUODI the fisherman comes out of the hut, WERNI the huntsman comes down from the rock, KUONI the herdsman comes carrying the milk pail on his shoulder. SEPPI, his apprentice, follows him.*)
RUODI: (*To JENNI.*)
Jenni, make speed and pull the boat to shore.
The weather's coming on, the mountain's cracking,
the Mytenstein is putting on its cloud,
and there's a cold wind blowing up from the pass.
Reckon the storm'll be on us 'fore we think.
KUONI: Rain's coming, ferryman. My sheep are eating
all the grass they can, and snow'll settle.
WERNI: Fish are jumping, and the coots are diving,
seems we're in for a storm, and quick approaching.
KUONI: (*To SEPPI.*)
Look out, young Seppi, see the stock don't wander.
SEPPI: There's Liesl, I can tell her by the bell.
KUONI: Then we're all right, she wanders off the furthest.
RUODI:
That's a fine set of bells you have there, master shepherd.
WERNI: And handsome stock – belongs to you, then, does it?
KUONI: I'm not that rich – my master, Attinghausen,
owns them and leases them to me.

RUODI: The band around the cow's neck suits it fine.

KUONI: She knows it too, seeing she leads the herd;

    if I took it back, she'd never graze again.

RUODI: Come on now! Can a beast that has no sense…?

WERNI: Easy to say. Beasts have got sense as well:

    something we soon find out from hunting chamois,

    they always have a sentinel when they

    go grazing who can warn them when there's danger.

RUODI: (*To KUONI.*)

    Are you for home now?

KUONI: Ay, the grass is grazed.

WERNI: Safe journey, herdsman.

KUONI: And the same to you.

    Journeys like yours don't always have safe endings.

RUODI: There's someone coming, running all he can.

WERNI: I know him. That is Baumgart from Alzellen.

    (*KONRAD BAUMGARTEN bursts in, out of breath.*)

BAUMGARTEN: For God's sake, Ferryman, give me your boat!

RUODI: No, now, what is the hurry, then?

BAUMGARTEN: Cast off!

    You're saving me from death! Row me across

KUONI: What is the matter, friend?

WERNI: Who's after you?

BAUMGARTEN: (*To RUODI.*)

    O, hurry, they are at my heels already!

    The Governor's horsemen are on my tracks

    and I am marked for death, if they should take me!

RUODI: Why are the horsemen following you, then?

BAUMGARTEN: First save me and I'll tell you everything.

WERNI: You've blood on you. What has been happening?

BAUMGARTEN:

    The Emperor's bailiff, the Governor in the Rossburg…

KUONI: Lord Wolfenschiess? Then, is he after you?

BAUMGARTEN: He'll do no more harm. I have killed him.

ALL: (*Drawing back.*)

    God have mercy on you! What have you done?

BAUMGARTEN: What any man in my place would have done.

    Exercised my rights as free householder

against the violator of my honour, and my wife's.

KUONI: Did the Governor attack your honour?

BAUMGARTEN: That he should fail to achieve his filthy plans
was left to God to hinder – and my axe.

WERNI: You mean you hit his head in with an axe?

KUONI: Now let us hear it all, it will take time
for him to get the boat free from the bank.

BAUMGARTEN: I was cutting wood in the forest, when my wife
came running to me, with the fear of death
upon her. The Governor was in my house,
he'd given orders to prepare a bath.
And then he'd made impossible demands
on her; but she'd escaped and come to find me.
Just as I was, I hurried home, and there
my axe made sure his bath held more than water.

WERNI: You did right, there is not a man would blame you.

KUONI: The villain! He has got what he deserved!
And long deserved by the folk of Unterwalden.

BAUMGARTEN:
But now the story has come out, they're after me –
while we stand talking – God – time's running out –
(*It begins to thunder.*)

KUONI: Quick, fisherman, take this honest man across.

RUODI: Not me. A fine old storm is brewing up.
He'll have to wait.

BAUMGARTEN: Dear God! I cannot wait.
Each minute of delay is costing me…

KUONI: (*To RUODI.*)
We must help our neighbours; this is the sort of thing
can happen any time, to any of us.
(*Thunder and rain.*)

RUODI: The wind is up, you see how high the sea is,
I cannot steer through waves and weather both.

BAUMGARTEN: (*Embracing his knees.*)
God be to you, as you are now to me –

WERNI: It's life and death, show pity, ferryman!

KUONI: He lives here, he has got a wife and children!
(*More thunder.*)

RUODI: What's that? I have a life to lose as well,
    wife and children too at home, like him – just look
    how rough it is, how the water stirs and hisses,
    think what the currents underneath are like.
    I should be glad to save the honest man,
    but it is just impossible, look yourselves.
BAUMGARTEN: Then I must fall into my enemies' hands,
    the shore of my salvation in my sight!
    It's over there! I can see it, plain,
    could shout out loud enough for them to hear,
    here is a boat could carry me across,
    and I must lie here, helpless and abandoned!
KUONI: Look, someone's coming!
WERNI: William Tell, from Buerglen.
    (*Enter TELL with crossbow.*)
TELL: Who is this man who's begging here for help?
KUONI: From Alzellen. In an affair of honour
    he killed the Governor of the castle, Wolfenschiess.
    The High Governor's men are after him,
    he begged the ferryman to row him across,
    but he was frightened of the storm, and wouldn't.
RUODI: Ask Tell then, he can steer a boat, like me,
    let him confirm, whether he'd dare the journey.
TELL: If you must do it, then you dare to do it.
    (*Violent claps of thunder. The water foams up.*)
RUODI: I have to dive into the jaws of Hell?
    Nobody would, who had a grain of sense.
TELL: A brave man thinks of himself the last of all.
    Have faith in God and save the persecuted.
RUODI: Easy to give advice safe on dry land.
    There is the boat and there's the lake. You try it!
TELL: The lake may show more mercy than the Governor:
    Try it, Boatman!
OTHERS: Save him! Save him! Save him!
RUODI: Not if he was my brother or my child,
    I couldn't do it, Simon and Judah's saints' day,
    the lake is raging for a sacrifice.

TELL: Nothing will be achieved with just fine words.

    Time is too short, the man needs help and now.

    Boatman, will you give it him?

RUODI: No, I shall not.

TELL: Then, in the name of God, give me the boat,

    and let me try what my poor strength can do.

KUONI: Tell, you're a brave man!

WERNI: And a fellow-huntsman!

BAUMGARTEN:

    You've saved my life, Tell, you're my guardian angel!

TELL: I may have saved you from the Governor's rage,

    another power must save you from the storm,

    better to fall into the hand of God,

    than that of Man.

    (*To KUONI.*) See my wife looked after,

    if I should meet with more than Man should meet with,

    I only did what I could not refuse.

    (*He springs into the boat.*)

KUONI: (*To RUODI.*)

    A master steersman you are. You can see

    what Tell dares do, and you can't follow him?

RUODI: There's better men than I that wouldn't do it:

    there's not two men like him in all the land.

WERNI: (*From up on the rocks.*)

    He's casting off. Then God be with you, swimmer!

    Look, how that little ship rides on the waves!

KUONI: (*On the shore.*)

    The torrent's hiding it – I can see no more –

    no, look! It's there again! With all his strength

    he's pulling her through the breakers. What a man!

SEPPI: The Governor's men are coming at full gallop.

KUONI: By God they are! Just got away in time!

    (*Enter a troop of Governor Landenberg's HORSEMEN.*)

FIRST HORSEMAN: Give us the murderer you are sheltering.

SECOND HORSEMAN: He came this way, no good denying it.

KUONI / RUODI: Who is it you mean?

FIRST HORSEMAN: (*Noticing the boat.*) What's that? Damnation!

WERNI: (*Above.*) Is he in the boat, the one you're looking for?
A turn of speed, and you can catch him up.
SECOND: Escaped! Damnation!
FIRST: (*To KUONI and RUODI.*) And you helped them to it.
You'll pay for this! Attack the village!
Tear down their hovels, burn them and destroy them!
(*They dash out.*)
SEPPI: (*Rushing after them.*)
My lambs!
KUONI: (*Following.*) Oh, God! My cattle!
WERNI: Ah, the villains!
RUODI: (*Wringing his hands.*)
Oh, God of justice, when will we find our saviour?

Scene 2

Steinen in Schwyz. By a lime tree in front of STAUFFACHER's
house on the Landstrasse, near the bridge.
WERNER STAUFFACHER enters in talk with PFEIFFER
of Lucerne.

PFEIFFER: I tell you, Stauffacher, you must not swear
loyalty to Austria, if you can avoid it.
Stay with the Empire, as you have till now,
and bravely stand with God by your old freedom!
(*Presses his hand sincerely and makes to go.*)
STAUFFACHER: Stay till my wife gets here. Here in Schwyz
you are my guest, as I'm yours in Lucerne.
PFEIFFER: My thanks! But I must reach Gersau tonight.
And what you have to suffer in the way
of greed and arrogance from your governors,
bear it with patience. Things may quickly change,
another emperor succeed to the throne,
but once you're Austria's, it is for ever.
(*He leaves. STAUFFACHER, concerned, sits under the lime*
tree. Here he is discovered by GERTRUD, his wife, who stands
watching him in silence for a while.)
GERTRUD: So serious, my friend? I hardly know you.
For some days now, I've watched you, and said nothing,

seen how your brow is creased with some dark worry.
There's some infirmity weighing on your heart,
which you should tell me; as a loving wife,
I can demand half of your sorrows too.
(*STAUFFACHER silently takes her hand.*)
What is it that's depressing you, oh, tell me.
All your hard work's rewarded, with a fortune,
the barns are full; so are the cattle-sheds,
the horses, groomed and grazed, are safely brought
down from the mountains to their winter stalls.
There stands your house, rich as a nobleman's,
newly constructed from the finest timber,
as you had planned, windows on every side,
and bright with painted coats of arms, and words
of wisdom for the traveller to read
and to digest in wonder at their worth.
STAUFFACHER: Well built, well organised the house may be,
    but oh! The ground we built on is unsteady.
GERTRUD: But Werner, tell me, what do you mean by that?
STAUFFACHER: I sat under this lime tree recently,
    thinking how satisfactory things all were.
    When suddenly the Governor, with his troops,
    rode by from his residence at Kuesnacht.
    He halted here, before the house, in wonder,
    but I got up at once, and as I should,
    in all humility approached the man
    who is the Emperor's representative
    here in this country. Then, 'Whose is this house?'
    he asked maliciously, since he knew quite well.
    Answering quickly, but discreetly, I replied:
    'This house, Lord Governor, is the Emperor's,
    my lord and yours, and held in fee by me.'
    'I am the Viceroy of the Emperor,'
    he said, 'and do not wish the peasantry
    to build according to their own devices,
    and live there just as if they owned the land.
    I therefore am forbidding it, in your case.'
    So saying, he rode defiantly away,

leaving me worried, thinking of his words.

GERTRUD: My lord and husband, will you let your wife
    give you a piece of frank, sincere advice?
    I count myself, with pride, a daughter of
    the noble Iberg, an experienced man.
    We sisters would sit spinning in the evenings
    while Father met with leading councillors,
    while they read documents of the old Emperor,
    debating soberly on the country's good.
    Paying attention, I head many words,
    what wise men thought and what good men desired,
    and I kept note of everything I heard.
    So listen to me, take heed of what I'm saying,
    I have known for a long time what it is that grieves you.
    The governor torments you, wants to harm you.
    You are a hindrance to him, since the Schwyzers
    will not swear fealty to the new royal house,
    but remain solidly behind the Empire,
    just as their ancestors have always done –
    is that not so? Or tell me I am lying!

STAUFFACHER: It's true. That is why Gessler so resents me.

GERTRUD: He envies you because you live at peace,
    a free man, living on the land you own.
    For he has none. You hold this house in fee
    from the Emperor himself, and you may show
    your fortune as he shows his provinces.
    For you need recognise no man your master
    up to the highest power in Christendom.
    The Governor is a younger son, with nothing
    that he can call his own except his title.
    He must see every citizen's good fortune
    with eyes askance and poisonous with envy.
    You he swore long ago to undermine –
    so far to no effect – but will you wait
    till he has gratified his evil will?
    The wise man acts ahead.

STAUFFACHER: What's to be done?

GERTRUD: Listen to my advice. You know that here

in Schwyz all honest men complain of
the greed and cruelty of this Governor.
You need be in no doubt that over there
in Uri and in Unterwalden they
are sick and tired as well of this oppression
(since Landenberg across the lake is quite
as harsh as Gessler here in his behaviour).
No fishing boat can come across without
some new tale of the bailiffs' cruelty.
That's why those among you who
have honest minds should gather and discuss
how you may rid yourselves of this misrule.
I'm confident God won't abandon you.
He will allow the righteous cause to triumph.
Have you no friend in Uri you could go to,
and honestly reveal what you are thinking?
STAUFFACHER: I do indeed know many brave men there,
and well-respected men of power too,
whose confidence I have, as they have mine.
(*He stands.*)
Wife, what a storm of dangerous trains of thought
have you awakened in my quiet mind!
My inmost thoughts you bring to light of day,
and things I silently suppressed, those thoughts
that I forbade myself, you just come out with
as if they were the least things in the world!
But have you thought what you are asking of me?
Discord and the clash of arms are what
you plan to bring into this peaceful valley.
Must we, a feeble people, farmers, shepherds,
make war against the master of the world?
All they are waiting for is an excuse
to hurl their armies at our wretched country
and exercise the right of conquerors,
under the cloak of 'civil discipline',
destroy the ancient charters of our freedom.
GERTRUD: But you are men as well, you know about
the wielding of an axe: God helps the brave.

STAUFFACHER: Wife, if you knew the horror that is war,
the havoc that it wreaks on herds and herdsmen…
GERTRUD: We must accept whatever Heaven sends.
A noble heart will not accept injustice.
STAUFFACHER:
This house that we have built here is your pride;
war is a dragon that would burn it down.
GERTRUD: If I believed my heart was tied to things
of this world, I would light the fire myself.
STAUFFACHER: Do you believe Humanity survives?
War will not spare the infant in the cradle.
GERTRUD: Innocence will have its friends in Heaven!
Look to the future, Werner, not the past!
STAUFFACHER: Men may die in battle, and with courage:
what sort of fate is there reserved for you?
GERTRUD: The weakest of us have a final choice.
Just jumping off that bridge would set me free.
STAUFFACHER: (*Falling into her arms.*)
If such a heart can beat within your breast,
you would fight for your hearth and home with joy,
and show no fear of any Kaiser's armies!
I shall immediately set off for Uri,
where I have a friend, Herr Walter Fuerst,
whose thoughts on these things are the same as mine.
There I shall also find the Banneret
von Attinghausen – though a nobleman,
he loves the people and the ancient customs.
With them I shall discuss the ways in which
we may resist the country's enemies.
Farewell, and while I am away, do you
shrewdly control the running of the house.
Give generously to the pilgrim, wandering
to the House of God, as to the holy monk,
collecting for his monastery, send them forth
well cared-for. Let our house not hide itself:
outside it faces on the main highway,
a hospitable roof for every wanderer.

(They are withdrawing into the background. Enter TELL with BAUMGARTEN.)

TELL: You have no further need now of my company,
go into that house; Stauffacher lives there,
a friend to the oppressed – but there he is!
(They go towards him, as the scene changes.)

Scene 3

Public Square in Altdorf, capital of Canton Uri.
On an elevation in the rear of the stage, a fortress is under construction, far enough advanced for the completed form to be apparent. The upstage side is completed, the front is still being worked on, the scaffolding still in place, on which workmen are climbing and descending; at the upper level are the tilermen. Everything is in motion, at work.

OVERSEER: *(Urging on the workmen, with his staff.)*
Come on, no loitering there. Bricks, lime, mortar,
load them and bring them! When the governor comes,
he'll want to see a little progress there.
It's like having a lot of snails to work.
(To two WORKMEN, with loads.)
Call that a load? Take as much again!
Good for nothing but shirking at the job!

WORKMAN: Bit hard to have to drag the stones together
that go to build a prison for ourselves.

OVERSEER: What's that? Complaints? It's a fine kind of people,
fit for nothing more than milking cows,
and lazing up and down the mountainsides.

OLD MAN: *(Taking a rest.)* I can't go on.

OVERSEER: *(Shaking him.)*
Come on, old man, get back to work with you!

WORKMAN: Haven't you any feelings, then, making him,
an old man who can hardly still stand upright,
making him do this kind of work, at his age?

STONEMASON and ASSISTANTS:
It's downright scandalous!

OVERSEER: Why don't you pay some mind
  to your own jobs, and let me get on with mine?

WORKMAN TWO:
  What'll they call this place when once it's finished?

OVERSEER:
  Fortress Uri. (*WORKMEN laugh.*) Oh, yes, what's so funny?

FIRST WORKMAN: This cottage, to control the whole of Uri?

SECOND WORKMAN: Try and see how many of these molehills
  you'll need to get a mountain like the lowest
  of any that you'll find up here in Uri!
  (*OVERSEER goes upstage.*)

STONEMASON: I'd like to throw the hammer in the lake
  I've had to use at work on this damned building!
  (*TELL and STAUFFACHER enter.*)

STAUFFACHER: I'd rather not have lived than look at this!

TELL: It's not good to be here. Let us go further.

STAUFFACHER: Am I in Uri – in the land of freedom?

STONEMASON: Sir, but you should have seen the cellars
  under the towers! Those who live in there
  will not be woke by cockcrow any more.

STAUFFACHER:
  Oh God!

STONEMASON: You see these buttresses, these bastions,
  built to last forever, you would think!

TELL: What hands have built, they can demolish, though!
  The house of Freedom is the work of God. (*Pointing to
  the mountains.*)
  (*A drum is heard beating. Enter men with a hat on a pole,
  followed by a PUBLIC ANNOUNCER, women and children
  following tumultuously.*)

FIRST WORKMAN:
  What is the drum for? Better take care!

STONEMASON: What is?
  The Carnival procession for – and why the hat?

ANNOUNCER: In the Name of His Imperial Majesty – attention!

WORKMEN: Quiet over there! What is he going to say?

ANNOUNCER: People of Uri, here you see this hat,
  which will be set up on a column in

153

the middle of Altdorf, the most prominent
position. The Lord Governor's will's as follows:
the hat is to receive the same respect
as he himself; it shall be honoured too
by heads uncovered and by bended knees –
His Majesty in this will see obedience.
Persons omitting these formalities will be
liable to the King with property and body.
(*The people laugh aloud, the drum is beaten, they cross the stage.*)

FIRST WORKMAN:

What new unheard-of thing is this the Governor
has thought up? Are we to salute a hat?
Did anybody ever hear the like?

STONEMASON: Bowing our knees before a hat! Is this
a joke to play on serious citizens?

FIRST WORKMAN: Even if it was the Imperial crown!
It's the hat of Austria, I saw it hanging
above the throne, when they were granting leaseholds!

STONEMASON: The hat of Austria! Then take care, it could
well be a trick to sell us to the Austrians!

WORKMEN: No patriot could stomach such disgrace.

STONEMASON: Come, let us discuss this with the others.
(*They go upstage.*)

TELL: (*To STAUFFACHER.*)

Well, now you know the facts. Goodbye, Herr Werner.

STAUFFACHER:

Where are you going? Don't hurry away from here.

TELL: My house is missing me. Fare you well.

STAUFFACHER: My heart is full; I need to speak with you.

TELL: A heavy heart is not made light with words.

STAUFFACHER: But words are what we need to preface deeds.

TELL: Patience and silence are all the deeds we need.

STAUFFACHER: Does that mean we must bear the unbearable?

TELL: The harshest tyrants have the shortest reigns.
When the Foehn wind rises from its caverns,
men put their fires out, ships make sail for harbour,
and the great gusts blow, harmless, without trace,
across the earth. Men live quiet in their homes.

Peace is assured to men of peace.

STAUFFACHER: You think so?

TELL: The serpent does not bite unless provoked.
In the end, they will be weary of themselves,
when they see the land at peace and quiet.

STAUFFACHER: We could do much if we could stand together.

TELL: With shipwreck it is 'every man for himself'.

STAUFFACHER: Could you desert a common cause so coldly?

TELL: We can only safely count upon ourselves.

STAUFFACHER: Banded together, even the weak are strong.

TELL: The strong man's at his strongest on his own.

STAUFFACHER:
Our desperate country cannot count on you, then,
if it resorts to arms in self-defence?

TELL: (*Gives him his hand.*)
Tell would save a lost lamb from a pit,
and is he someone to desert his friends?
Just leave me out of your deliberations,
on what to do, I'm not for such a task.
But if you need me for specific action,
then call on Tell, all you need do is ask.
(*They go off on different sides. A sudden uproar round the scaffolding.*)

STONEMASON: (*Hurrying over.*) What is it?

FIRST WORKMAN: (*Comes forward, shouts.*) The tiler. He fell off the roof.
(*Enter BERTA von BRUNECK, with ATTENDANTS.*)

BERTA: (*Bursting in.*)
Is he hurt badly? Hurry, save him, help him –
if it is possible, save him – here is money…
(*Throwing valuables among the people.*)

TILER: Money! For you the universal answer.
When you have torn the father from his children,
the husband from his wife, when you have brought
torment on all the world, you think you can
make it all up again with money – get away!
This was a happy land, before you came,
you left the door wide open to Despair.

155

BERTA: (*To the OVERSEER, who comes back.*)
Will he live? (*OVERSEER shakes his head.*)
Accursed fortress, built
with curses, and lived in by none but curses!
(*Exit.*)

Scene 4

WALTER FUERST's house.
WALTER FUERST and ARNOLD von MELCHTAL enter
severally.

MELCHTAL: Herr Walter Fuerst –
FUERST: If we were overheard!
Stay where you are. Their spies are everywhere.
MELCHTAL: Have you brought me no news from Unterwalden?
Nothing from my father? I cannot
idly live here like a prisoner.
What have I done so criminal that I
should be kept hidden like a murderer?
An insolent boy, who came and took my oxen,
my best team he was going to drive away
before my very eyes, on the Governor's orders…
I broke his fingers for him with my stick.
FUERST: You were too quick. He was the Governor's man,
despatched by higher Authority, and you
by quarrelling, made yourself the guilty party,
and you must pay the price, however steep.
MELCHTAL: I had to listen to his insolent tongue
telling me: 'If the peasant wants his bread,
he'll have to go and draw the plough himself.'
It cut me to the soul to see the boy
unspan those beautiful beasts out of the shafts;
they were lowing indistinctly, just as if
they felt the injustice, lunging with their horns.
That was when my anger overtook me:
no longer master of myself, I struck him.
FUERST: Oh, when we barely can control our own hearts,
how do we tame the hearts of eager youth?

MELCHTAL: My one concern is for my father – he
    needs caring for, and his son is far away.
    The Governor hates him, as he always fought
    honourably for Freedom and the Right.
    And for that reason they will harass him,
    with no one there to shield him from such treatment.
    Come to me what may, I must go back.
FUERST: Just wait a while; possess yourself in patience
    until some news can get to us from there.
    There's knocking, go on in – you are not safe
    in Uri from the Landesberger men,
    these tyrants hold their hands out to each other.
MELCHTAL: Teaching us what we should do.
FUERST: Now go!
    I'll call you back here, when the coast is clear.
    (*MELCHTAL goes in.*)
    Unhappy boy, I can't confess to him
    the dark presentiments I have – who's knocking there?
    The least noise at the door makes me suspect
    some mischief, treachery in every corner.
    The agents of the mighty penetrate
    into the inmost corners of the houses,
    soon we'll need bolts and bars on every door.
    (*He opens the door and steps back in astonishment as Werner
    STAUFFACHER comes in.*)
    What do I see? By God! A valued guest!
    No better man has ever crossed my threshold.
    Welcome, Herr Werner, welcome to my house!
    What brings you here? What do you want in Uri?
STAUFFACHER: (*Holding out his hand.*)
    Old days, old ways, old Switzerland.
FUERST: You bring them
    here with you – see, the mere sight of you
    fills my heart with warmth – sit down, sit down!
    How did you leave Frau Gertrud, your good wife,
    the estimable daughter of wise Iberg?
    No traveller from Germany to Italy
    that does not praise the hospitality

of your house – but now tell me, did you come
direct from Fluelen? Did you not cast your eyes
aside at anything before arriving here?

STAUFFACHER: (*Sitting.*) I did see one astonishing new work
in progress, which I cannot say I cared for.

FUERST: Friend, you have hit it at a single glance.

STAUFFACHER: Never in the history of Uri
has there been such a prison, such a fortress,
nor dungeon as constricted as the grave.

FUERST: The grave of Liberty. You have the name.

STAUFFACHER: I will not hide from you, Herr Walter Fuerst,
it was not idle curiosity
that brought me here, but pressing, real concern.
Persecution I had left at home,
but now I find such persecution here as well.
What we are suffering is not to be borne,
nor is there any end to it in sight.
The Swiss have been, time out of mind, accustomed
to freedom, good relations with their neighbours.
This sort of thing's unknown here, not since shepherds
first drove their flocks to graze up on these mountains.

FUERST: You're right, it is unheard of, what they're doing
the noble Herr von Attinghausen, who
can still remember living in the old days,
finds it no longer to be tolerated.

STAUFFACHER: And things are bad out there in Unterwalden,
and bloodily accounted for – the Emperor's man,
Wolfenschiess, then living on the Rossberg,
suddenly fancied some forbidden fruit,
Baumgarten's wife (they live in Alzellen).
He wanted to impose on her some mischief,
only her husband felled him with an axe.

FUERST: God's judgements are most just. Did you say
Baumgarten? A most reasonable man.
Did he escape? And has he been well hidden?

STAUFFACHER: Your son-in-law brought him across the lake,
and he is safely at my house in Steinen.
The same man told me of a far worse case

happening in Sarnen, for which the heart
of any fellow-countryman must bleed.

FUERST: (*Alerted.*)

Go on. Tell me.

STAUFFACHER: In Melchtal, by the entry into Kerns,
lives a just man called Heinrich von der Halden,
a voice of influence in the community.

FUERST: Who doesn't know him! What of him! Speak out!

STAUFFACHER: The Governor, in punishment for some
minor infraction of his son's, decreed
the confiscation of his finest pair
of oxen, and unyoked them from the plough.
The boy then struck the servant down, and fled.

FUERST: (*In extreme tension.*)

The father though – how are things with him?

STAUFFACHER: The Governor demanded of the father
he should produce his son, in front of him,
and when the father swore with perfect truth,
not to have had a word of news from him,
the Governor then called in the torturers…

FUERST: (*Jumping up and trying to lead him to the other side of the
room.*) Oh, hush, no more!

STAUFFACHER: (*His voice rising.*) 'The son may have escaped,
I still have you!' – he had him thrown to the ground,
and sharp steel probes were driven into his eyes –

FUERST: Merciful Heavens!

MELCHTAL: (*Bursting in.*)   Did you say his eyes?

STAUFFACHER: (*Astonished, to FUERST.*)

Who is this boy?

MELCHTAL: (*Grasping him violently.*) Did you say his eyes?

FUERST: Oh, God, how pitiable!

STAUFFACHER: Who is this?

(*At a gesture from FUERST.*)

Is it the son? Oh, God in Heaven!

MELCHTAL: And I

must be away from there! In both his eyes?

FUERST: Control yourself, and take it like a man.

MELCHTAL: The fault was mine, the punishment should have
   been mine! Really blind, completely blinded?
STAUFFACHER: I'm telling you; the source of light is gone.
   He'll never see the light of day again.
FUERST: Ease his suffering!
MELCHTAL: Never! Never again!
   (*He presses his hand to his eyes and is silent for a while, then,
   turning from one to another, he speaks quietly, his voice choked
   with tears.*)
   The gift of sight – the noblest of Heaven!
   All creatures live from light, each fortunate species,
   the plants themselves turn joyfully towards it.
   And he must sit there, groping, in the night,
   eternal darkness, never more to be
   revived by glowing flowers, meadows' green,
   never more to see the mountain snows…
   To die is nothing – to live, though, and not see,
   that is misfortune – why do you look at me
   so pitifully? My two healthy eyes,
   and I cannot give one to my blind father,
   not one faint shimmer from the sea of light,
   that blazing blindingly fills up my vision!
STAUFFACHER: I have to magnify your great distress,
   instead of lessening it – there's worse to come.
   The Governor has taken everything
   he had, and left him nothing but a stick
   to wander, naked, blind, from door to door.
MELCHTAL: All that was left the blind old man – a stick!
   Everything taken – even the light of day,
   the birthright of the very poorest! Now,
   not a word more of staying hidden here!
   What sort of wretched coward must I be?
   To think of my own safety, and not yours –
   leaving your dear head as guarantee
   in the hands of that bloody man. Now an end
   to cowardly precautions! Nothing but
   bloody revenge is in my thoughts – I shall
   go back, and no one shall prevent me now –

demand my father's eyesight from the Governor –
let him hide in the furthest ranks of his soldiers,
I shall find him out – Life has no more for me,
unless this hot, sharp, monstrous pain inside me,
is cooled in his life's blood forever.
(*He makes to go.*)

FUERST: Wait!
What can you do against him? He sits safe
in Sarnen in his fortress and makes fun
of impotent fury, shielded in his stronghold.

MELCHTAL: Whether he lives in the icy fortress of
the Schreckhorn, or still higher, where the Jungfrau
has sat veiled since Eternity began –
I shall find my way to him, and a score
of young, like-minded men, we'll smash his fortress.
And if there's none to follow me, if all
of you, too scared about your huts and herds,
bend your necks to the tyrant's yoke, then I
will summon the shepherds from the mountains, where,
under the open sky, where hearts and minds
are fresher, healthier, I can relate
the manner of these happenings to them.

STAUFFACHER: (*To FUERST.*)
This is his high point – should we not first wait
until the extremer limits –

MELCHTAL: What extreme
remains still to be feared, if our very eyes
are not safe in their sockets any longer?
And are we so defenceless? We have learned
to bend the crossbow and to bear the weight
of the battle-axe. And why? Every creature has
a weapon to be used in desperation:
the stag at bay will show its much-feared horns;
the chamois drags the hunter to the abyss;
even the ox, the peaceful friend of men,
who patiently bends his mighty neck beneath
the plough, springs up, in anger, sharpening

his powerful horn, and flings his enemy
into the clouds.

FUERST: If the three cantons thought
    like the three of us, something might be achieved.

STAUFFACHER: If Uri calls, with Unterwalden's aid,
    Schwyz will be faithful to the old alliance

MELCHTAL: In Unterwalden I have many friends,
    each one would shed his flesh and blood with joy,
    if he were ranked alongside the others.
    Oh, venerable fathers of this land!
    I stand between you here, with all your great
    experience, and I am only young –
    in council I should keep a modest silence.
    But do not, for my youth and inexperience,
    reject with scorn my words or my advice.
    It is not youthful, heated blood that drives me,
    but the agonising power of deep distress,
    to which even the rock face must show pity.
    You are both fathers, heads of families,
    in which you each wish a courageous son,
    to give due honour to the hairs of your heads,
    and keep a holy watch upon your sight.
    Oh, since you yourselves have not yet suffered
    these things, since your eyes, still fresh and bright,
    move in their orbits, do not, though, for that
    make yourselves strangers to our real need.
    The tyrant's sword hangs over your heads too,
    you have withdrawn your loyalty to Austria,
    that was my father's only crime, and you
    should share both guilt and condemnation with him.

STAUFFACHER: (*To FUERST.*)
    You must decide! I am prepared to follow.

FUERST: Let us hear first what Herr von Sillinen
    and Herr von Attinghausen would advise –
    their names, I think, should win us friends enough.

MELCHTAL: Where is there in the cantons here a name
    more honourable than your own, or yours?
    People will trust the sterling quality

of names like yours, they sound well in the country.
You both inherited a rich estate
and made them richer – do we need the gentry?
Let us complete our enterprise on our own.
What if we were truly on our own?
I think we'd know how to defend ourselves.

STAUFFACHER: The nobles have not yet experienced
the same emergency as we. The flood
that rages lower down has not yet reached
their level, but their aid will not be lacking
once they have seen the country up in arms.

FUERST: Were there some arbitrator who could judge
between us and Austria, this could go to law.
But our oppressor is the Emperor
himself, our highest judge – so, God must help us
through our own right arms. Sound out the men of Schwyz
and I shall find what friends we have in Uri.
But who are we to send to Unterwalden?

MELCHTAL: Send me. Whom does it concern more closely?

FUERST: I cannot. As you are my guest, I must
guarantee your safety.

MELCHTAL: Let me go!
I know the secret roads, the mountain paths,
I shall find friends enough, who will be able
to hide me, and be willing to give me shelter.

STAUFFACHER: Let him go with God, for over there
there are no traitors – tyranny is so
despised, it cannot find the tools to work through.
Baumgarten can find us allies too
in nid dem Wald, and stir the land to action.

MELCHTAL: How can we bring our known good friends together
without arousing the suspicions of
the tyrants?

STAUFFACHER: We could assemble at the harbour mouth,
by the basins where the merchant ships tie up.

FUERST: We cannot go to work so openly.
Hear what I think. North-west of the lake,
going to Brunnen, opposite the rock,

there is a meadow hidden in the forest,
known by the shepherd people as the Ruetli
(because the woodland there has been uprooted).
(*To MELCHTAL.*)
It's where your lands and ours both share a frontier,
(*To STAUFFACHER.*)
and is for you an easy water-crossing.
We make our way there by neglected tracks
by night, and we can talk there at our leisure.
Each of us can bring ten trusted men
of the same heart and mind as we ourselves:
we can then discuss together what
concerns us all together, and with God
we can decide upon these things afresh.

STAUFFACHER: So be it. Now give me your honest hands,
and so! As we three men here clasp our hands
together, openly, without false hearts,
let us stand, in both defiance and defence,
together for the sake of Life and Death.

FUERST / MELCHTAL: Life and Death!

(*They stand for some moments in silence, their hands enlaced.*)

MELCHTAL: Oh, my blind, old father!
You can no longer see the day of Freedom,
but you shall hear of it – when the fire-beacons
flame up from mountain peak to mountain peak,
the mighty castles of the tyrants crumble,
in their poor huts your peasants growl and rumble,
they bring you the great news, and your dark night
will die away, in beam on beam of light.

End of Act One.

ACT TWO

Scene 1

Mansion of Freiherr von ATTINGHAUSEN. A Gothic hall ornamented with coats of arms and helmets.
The Freiherr, an old man of eighty-five, of tall and noble bearing, stands with a stick, on which is a chamois horn, and is wearing a fur doublet.
The shepherd, KUONI, and six other workmen with rakes and scythes are standing grouped.
ULRICH von RUDENZ enters, in knight's costume.

RUDENZ: Grandfather, I am here – what did you wish?
ATTINGHAUSEN:

 Let me first take my morning-draught with my men,
 after the ancient custom of our house.
 (*He drinks from a beaker, which then makes the round.*)
 Time was I'd be abroad in field and forest,
 keeping their industry and effort in my eye,
 just as my standard led them into battle.
 Now I am no more than steward here,
 and if the sun will not come here to warm me,
 I cannot go and seek it on the mountain.
 And so it is, through ever-narrower rooms
 I move, and slowly, to the narrowest
 and last of all, where life itself stands still:
 Now just my shadow, soon only my name.
KUONI: (*Bringing the beaker to RUDENZ.*)
 I'll bring it, Junker.
 (*Since RUDENZ hesitates to take the cup.*)
       Drink then! It has come
 out of one single vessel, and one heart.
ATTINGHAUSEN:

 Off with you now, my boys, and, come this evening,
 we can discuss the business of the country.
 (*The men go out.*)
 I see you girt and armoured, does this mean
 you mean to go to Altdorf, to the Herrenburg?

RUDENZ: Yes, grandfather, nor can I stay here longer –

ATTINGHAUSEN: (*Sitting.*)

> In such a hurry? Why? Is a young man's time
> so miserly laid out, that you must save it at
> the expense of seeing your old grandfather?

RUDENZ: I see you have no further need of me,

> I am a stranger here in my own house.

ATTINGHAUSEN: (*After a long, searching look at him.*)

> I am afraid you are. Your native country
> has become foreign to you – Uli! Uli!
> I do not know you now. You prance in silk,
> you flaunt the peacock feathers here with pride,
> and drape the purple cloak over your shoulders.
> Your countrymen you look at with contempt,
> treating his cordial greeting now with shame.

RUDENZ: Such honour as belongs to him, I pay him;

> the rights he abrogates, those I refuse him.

ATTINGHAUSEN: The king's severest anger lies upon

> the country – every patriotic heart
> is grieved at the tyrannic power
> that we endure – you alone remain
> unmoved by all the suffering – you are seen
> as being a deserter from your own,
> and siding with the national enemy,
> scorning our pain for the sake of easy pleasure,
> currying favour with the princes, while
> our country bleeds to death from all her wounds.

RUDENZ: The country is hard pressed – but why is that?

> Who is it tipped it into this distress?
> It would cost nothing but a simple word
> to free us from this misery in a moment,
> and bring the emperor to the way of mercy.
> Woe to those that bind the people's eyes,
> so they resist what's truly good for them.
> They are preventing, for their own advantage,
> the forest cantons swearing loyalty
> to Austria, as all the rest have done.
> It does them good, to sit there with the nobles

upon the upper bench – the Emperor
they want as master, so they'll have no master.
ATTINGHAUSEN: Must I hear this? And must I hear you say it?
RUDENZ: It was you challenged me, now let me finish.
What character are you playing, grandfather?
Does your pride go no higher than to be
provincial gentry and commander, ruling
next to a race of shepherds? Is that it?
Would it not be a more distinguished choice
to pay the homage due a royal master,
attach yourself to the splendour of his household,
rather than stay the equal of your servants,
sitting on the judgment bench with peasants?
ATTINGHAUSEN: Oh, Uli, Uli! I can hear the voice
of that seduction which has gained your ear:
it is poisoning your very heart!
RUDENZ: Yes, I'll not hide the fact – deep in my soul
I feel the mockery of foreigners, who call
us 'peasant nobles' – neither can I bear
to see all the young nobles hereabouts,
gathering glory under the Hapsburg standard,
while I must idle here on my estate,
losing the springtime of my life in drudgery.
Elsewhere things are happening, there is,
upon the other side of our mountains,
a shining world of fame out there in motion.
My helmet and my shield rust in the hall,
the battle-trumpet's brave, inspiring sound,
the herald's call that summons to the lists,
none of these will reach the valleys here,
only the cattle-call, monotony,
the noise of cowbells – all I ever hear.
ATTINGHAUSEN: Blinded and seduced by vapid shows!
Despise your native land! And be ashamed
of the ancient, pious customs of your father!
The time will come when you, with bitter tears,
will long to see the mountains of your home.
And that old cattle-call you so disdain,

it will enfold you in the pain of longing
when you remember it on foreign soil.
Love of one's country is a powerful force!
The strange, false world outside is not for you!
At the emperor's proud court, with your true heart,
you'll always be a stranger to yourself.
The world demands a different set of values
from those you have acquired here in the valleys.
Go, auction off your independent spirit,
take land in fief; become a prince's hireling,
since you can be an autocrat at home,
a prince in your own right, on your own land.
Oh, Uli! Uli! Stay here with your own!
Don't go to Altdorf – do not leave behind
the holy place that is your fatherland! –
I am the last to bear my name. My line
will end with me. My helm and shield hang there,
and they will join me in the grave. Must I
draw my last breath in the thought that you
are only waiting for my eyes to dim,
for you to hurry off to hold in fee,
to have from Austria what I had from God !
RUDENZ: It is in vain that we resist the King:
the world is in his hands. Are we to show
persistent stubbornness in separating
the chain of lands with which he has so firmly
surrounded us? The markets and the law courts
belong to him; the trade routes and the very
pack-animals that trail up the St Gotthard
must all pay toll to him. His territories
are like a net enmeshing us, imprisoning.
And will the Empire help us? Can it help
itself against the growing Austrian power?
Where God can give no aid, nor can a Kaiser.
What confidence is in the Emperor's word
if, in financial, or military need,
towns that have sought protection of the Empire,
may be put up for sale or pawned by it?

No, grandfather! It is sense, wisdom and caution,
in these hard times of party politics,
we must attach ourselves to one strong head.
The Imperial crown will change from head to head,
it has no memory of loyal service.
But serve a powerful dynasty, and you
sow seed on fertile ground.

ATTINGHAUSEN: Are you so wise?
Would you see clearer than your noble fathers
who fought with heroes' strength, and blood and land
to save the invaluable jewel of Freedom?
Sail down to Lucerne, and ask them there
just how the power of Austria weighs them down.
And come they will, to count our herds and flocks,
survey our mountains, and preserve our game
in our free forests, and impose their turnpikes
upon our bridges, at our city gates.
Our poverty will pay for all their land
just as our blood will pay for all their wars.
No, if our blood is going to be shed,
let it be shed for us! The price of Freedom
is cheaper than the cost of slavery!

RUDENZ: And what are we to do, a race of shepherds,
against the armies of the mighty Albrecht?

ATTINGHAUSEN:
Learn what this 'race of shepherds' is, my boy!
I know them, they're a race I've led in battle,
a race that I saw fighting at Faenza...
Just let them try and force on us a yoke
which we decide that we shall not accept!
Oh, learn to feel whose blood flows in your veins!
And do not throw the true pearls of your worth
away on empty trifles and on tinsel –
lead a free people, one that cleaves to you
from heartfelt love, stands by you faithfully
in battle and in death – and let that be
your pride, and that be your nobility –
bind fast the alliances you were born to,

169

bind yourself to the fatherland, that dear land,
use your whole heart to hold it in your hands.
Here are the roots that feed you all your strength,
there in the outside world you are alone,
a hollow reed, a prey to every storm.
Come, we have not seen you for a long while,
try just one day with us – and for today
don't go to Altdorf – d'you hear me? Not today
a single day to spare for what is yours!
(*He clasps his hand.*)

RUDENZ: I gave my word – no, let me – I am bound...

ATTINGHAUSEN: (*Letting go of his hand, seriously.*)
You're bound – indeed you are, unhappy boy,
but not by word or oath, no, by love's ropes!
(*RUDENZ turns away.*)
Hide yourself all you please. But it is she,
Berta von Bruneck, it is she who draws you
to the Herrenburg, and fetters you
to the Emperor's service. You aim to win
the noble heiress at the price of your
defection from the country – but do not
deceive yourself! The bride-to-be is bait
set out to attract you, but she is not
destined for the companion of your innocence.

RUDENZ: I've heard enough. I bid farewell to you. (*Exit.*)

ATTINGHAUSEN: Distracted boy, stay here! – No, he has gone!
I cannot keep him here, nor can I save him –
so he deserts the Wolfenschiess' land –
Other young men will follow in his footsteps,
drawn by the charm of what is strange to them.
Oh, it was truly an unhappy moment
when the stranger first came to these quiet valleys,
to the destruction of our godly customs!
The new, with might, invades us, while the old,
the valuable steps down, other times are here,
another race of thinkers rules the world!
What am I doing here? They are all gone,
those men with whom I lived and ruled my life.

My day has been already buried deep:
happy they who do not need to live the new day!

Scene 2

*A meadow surrounded by high rocks and woods. In the rock are
hewn steps, platforms, and ladders down which the countrymen
can be seen descending. In the background is the lake, over which
at the beginning can be seen a moon-rainbow. High mountains
close off the view, behind them are visible the still higher ice peaks
of Glarus. It is deep night onstage; only the lake and glaciers
shine in the moonlight.*

*MELCHTAL, BAUMGARTEN, Struth von WINKELRIED,
Meier von SARNEN, Burkhardt am BUEHEL, Arnold von
SEWA, Klaus von der FLUEE and four OTHERS, all in
arms.*

MELCHTAL: (*Still offstage.*)
 The mountain track starts here. Just follow me.
 I know the rockface, and the shrine on top,
 we have arrived, this is the Ruetli.
 (*They enter with storm lanterns.*)
WINKELRIED: Listen!
SEWA: No one.
MEIER: Nobody has arrived yet. We Unterwaldeners
 are the first to get here.
MELCHTAL: How far gone's the night?
BAUMGARTEN: The watch in Selisberg has just called two.
 (*A bell is heard ringing in the distance.*)
MEIER: Listen!
BUHEL: The mattins bell from the forest chapel,
 sounding quite clearly over here from Schwyz.
FLUEE: The air is clear and so the sound can carry.
MELCHTAL: Some of you go and gather up some brushwood,
 so there's a fire going when the others come.
 (*Two MEN go out.*)
SEWA: It's a fine moonlit night. The lake is calm.
 Like a mirror.
BUHEL: They'll have easy sailing.

WINKELRIED: (*Pointing in the direction of the lake.*) Look!
Over there! Don't you see?

MEIER: See what? – Oh, yes!
A rainbow, in the middle of the night!

MELCHTAL: It is the moonlight makes it seem like that.

FLUEE: A strange and wonderful phenomenon.
Plenty alive now never saw the like.

SEWA: It's double, look! A paler one above it.

BAUMGARTEN: A boat's just setting out there.

MELCHTAL: That will be
Stauffacher. Never one to keep us waiting.
(*Goes to the shore with BAUMGARTEN.*)

MEIER: The men from Uri make us wait the longest.

BUHEL: They have to make a detour through the mountains,
the only way to avoid the Governor's scouts.
(*Meanwhile the two MEN have lit a fire in the middle of the
place.*)

MELCHTAL: (*On the shore.*)
Who goes there? The password!

STAUFFACHER: (*From below.*)   Friends to this land!
(*All go upstage, towards the new arrivals. Out of the boat come
STAUFFACHER, Itel REDING, Hans auf der MAUER, Joerg
im HOFE, Konrad HUNN, Ulrich der SCHMIED, Jost von
WEILER, and three further MEN, all similarly armed.*)

ALL: (*Shout.*) Welcome!!
(*While the others stay in the background, greeting one another,
MELCHTAL and STAUFFACHER come forward.*)

MELCHTAL: Oh, Herr Stauffacher! I have
seen him once more, who can no more see me!
Laid my hands on his eyes, and drawn a feeling,
from the dead sun of his glance, of blazing vengeance.

STAUFFACHER: Do not revenge what has already happened.
It is the threatening danger we must meet.
Now say, what progress you in Unterwalden
have made in the common cause, how do the people
see things, how have you yourself been able
to escape the tangled web of treachery?

MELCHTAL: Crossing the mountain range of the Surennes,

the widespread, desert, icy plateaus where
the harsh cry of the lammergeier sounds,
I reached the Alpine meadow where the shepherds
of Engelberg and Uri graze their flocks
in common, slaking my thirst in glacier-water,
which runs in foam along the watercourses.
I made free of the lonely summer cabins,
my own guest, my own landlord, till I came
to buildings happily inhabited.
These valleys had already had the news
of all the latest horrors, and my story
brought me devout respect and sympathy
at every door I knocked at on my way.
These honest souls I found had been appalled
at the tyrannical new rule imposed:
just as the Alps bring, year after year,
the same plants to flower, as their wells
are all the same, just as the clouds, the winds
follow unchangeably the same directions,
so are the ancient customs handed down
from grandfather to grandson, all unchanged.
They do not tolerate new-fangled change
to their old-accustomed, even way of life.
Their hardened hands were all held out to me,
down from the walls they reached the rusty swords,
and from their eyes blazed out a glowing courage
as I repeated those names over, which
those mountain people hold in veneration,
your own, and Walter Fuerst's – whatever you
think right to do, those things they swore to do,
they swore that they would follow you to death.
This was how I went from farm to farm
under the shield of hospitality –
and when I came into our native valley,
where family members live, widely scattered,
when I found my father, robbed and blind,
living on charity, on the mercy of
kind-hearted people, I –

STAUFFACHER: Dear God in Heaven!

MELCHTAL: I did not weep. I did not pour the strength
    of my distress out uselessly, in tears.
    Deep inside me, like a priceless treasure,
    I shut it in and only thought of action.
    I crept through all the windings of the mountain,
    no valley so obscure but I was in it.
    Right to the glacier's ice-covered foot,
    I looked for, and I found some habitation,
    and everywhere my wandering carried me,
    I found the selfsame hatred for the tyrants,
    for right up to this last frontier of all
    animate creation, where the stubborn earth
    gave out, the Governor's greed still robbed and stole –
    I used the power of words to be a powerful goad
    to rouse the feelings of these honest people,
    so that with heart and mind, they now are ours.

STAUFFACHER: You have achieved much in so short a time.

MELCHTAL: But I did more. There are two fortresses
    the countrymen particularly fear,
    Rossberg and Sarnen, where the enemy
    hides himself easily and safely in
    his walls of stone, from which he enslaves the land.
    Wanting to see it all with my own eyes,
    I went to Sarnen and there saw the castle.

STAUFFACHER: You dared set foot inside the tiger's lair?

MELCHTAL: I went there as a pilgrim, in disguise,
    I saw the Governor revelling at table:
    judge if I could force myself to see
    the enemy and not to strike him dead.

STAUFFACHER: Fortune then was surely on your side.
    (*Meanwhile the other COUNTRYMEN have come forward,
    close to the two.*)
    But tell me now who are the friends, and who
    the honest men who follow you? Make me
    acquainted with them, so that we may share
    our confidences, open-heartedly.

MEIER: Who, in the three cantons, does not know you?
My name is Meier von Sarnen, and this man
Beside me, Struth von Winkelried, my nephew.
STAUFFACHER: The name you mention is not strange to me.
It was a Winkelried who slew the dragon
at Weiler, in the marsh, and lost his life
in that encounter.
MEIER: An ancestor, Herr Werner.
MELCHTAL: (*Indicating two MEN.*)
These live beyond the forest, in the cloister
of Engelberg – they should not be despised
for being vassals, not, like us, free men
sitting on our hereditary estates –
they love this country, and are well-qualified.
STAUFFACHER: (*To both of them.*)
Give me your hands. Fortunate the man
who owes no bodily service on this earth,
and honour may be found in every class.
KONRAD HUNN: This is Herr Reding, our provincial councillor.
MEIER: I know Herr Reding. He's my adversary
in a case disputing an inheritance –
Herr Reding, we are enemies at law,
but here we are as one. (*Shakes his hand.*)
STAUFFACHER: Well, bravely spoken.
WINKELRIED:
You hear? They're coming. That was the horn of Uri.
(*To left and right, armed MEN, carrying storm lanterns, can be
see coming down the rock-face.*)
MAUER: Look! Isn't that the man of God himself,
the worthy pastor, coming down with them?
He does not fear the hard path nor the night,
there's a true shepherd, caring for his flock.
BAUMGARTEN:
Then there's the sexton, and Herr Walter Fuerst.
But I cannot see Tell in all that crowd.
(*WALTER FUERST, ROESSELMANN the pastor,
PETERMANN the sexton, KUONI the shepherd, WERNI
the huntsman, RUODI the fisherman, and five OTHERS; all*

together, thirty-three in number, they step forward, placing themselves around the fire.)

FUERST: This, then, is how we have to creep together,
on our own land, on our paternal earth,
like murderers, in the night, which wraps its cloak
round criminals and conspirators who dread
the sun, to claim what is our right, which speaks
louder and is as plain, as clear as day.

MELCHTAL: Let it be so. What the dark night has spun
shall soon lie clear and open to the sun.

ROESSELMANN:
Hear what God tells me, comrades, in my heart!
We are here in place of a national committee
and we can fairly claim to represent a people.
Let us proceed then after the ancient customs
as we have always done in quieter times;
let the emergency excuse whatever
may be illegal in this gathering.
Where right is exercised, then God is there,
and we are gathered here, under His Heaven.

STAUFFACHER:
Good, then we shall proceed by ancient custom;
It is still night, then let our right shine out.

MELCHTAL: And if our number's not complete, the heart
of a whole people is, the best of whom are with us.

HUNN: And if we do not have the ancient books
to hand, they are written fully, in our hearts.

ROESSELMANN: Then let the circle be at once completed,
And let us plant the swords of our authority.

MAUER: And let the councillor assume his place,
and let his sergeant stand there at his side!

PETERMANN: Three cantons are here represented. Which
of them should be declared head of this council?

MEIER: Let Schwyz and Uri both contest this honour,
we from Unterwalden will stand back.

MELCHTAL: We shall withdraw, we are the plaintiffs here,
who beg assistance from their powerful friends.

STAUFFACHER: Let Uri take the sword then, since their flag
   has gone before us in the imperial wars.
FUERST: The honour of the sword belongs to Schwyz,
   we are proud to share her race with her.
ROESSELMANN: Let me decide this friendly competition:
   Schwyz leads in council, Uri in the field.
FUERST: (*Handing the swords to STAUFFACHER.*) Take them!
STAUFFACHER: This honour's not for me, but for the oldest.
HOFE: Ulrich the Smith would be the oldest here.
MAUER: A sterling man indeed, but not a free one.
   No vassal can become a judge in Schwyz.
STAUFFACHER:
   Is not Herr Reding here, our old canton commander?
   How can we look for anyone more worthy?
FUERST: Let him preside here and direct this meeting!
   All those in favour here, then raise your hands.
   (*All raise their right hands.*)
REDING: (*Stepping into the middle.*)
   I cannot lay my hand upon the books,
   so I shall swear, by the eternal stars of night,
   I shall not swerve from what I hold is right.
   (*The two swords are set up in front of him. The circle forms
   around him, those from Schwyz in the centre, Uri on the right,
   Unterwalden on the left. He stands supported on his sword.*)
   What is it draws us all together here
   all three mountain peoples, to the bleak
   and desolate lakeside, in the dead of night?
   What is the content of this new alliance
   that we are forging here beneath the stars?
STAUFFACHER: This is no new alliance we are forging:
   an age-old contract from our fathers' time,
   we are renewing here. For, know this, comrades!
   Whether the mountains, or the lake divide us,
   whether each of our peoples rules itself,
   we all are of one race, and of one blood,
   and it is from one country that we came.
WINKELRIED: So it is true, then, what the old songs tell us,
   that came into this land from far away?

Then tell us everything you know of it,
so our new league is strengthened by the old.
STAUFFACHER: This is the way the ancient shepherds tell it.
Once a great people, far off in the North,
suffered great scarcity and harsh privation.
In this emergency it was decided
every tenth citizen, drawn by lot, should leave
the land of his fathers – and that is what happened!
With lamentation, men and women left
the country in a great procession going
southwards, hacking with their swords a path
through all the German lands until they came
into the high ground of this forest region.
Nor did the spirit of their progress ebb,
before they found themselves in that wild valley,
where now the river Muotta runs through meadows…
No trace of human beings could be seen,
but for one hut, stood lonely by the bank.
A man lived there, attending to the ferry –
but the lake was stormy and not navigable;
they therefore looked more carefully at the land,
and found it full of timber, and discovered
excellent springs, enough to make them think
they found themselves back once again at home.
And so they stayed, and built the ancient land
of Schwyz, going through many arduous times,
freeing the forest from its widespread roots.
and when the number of the people rose
more than the land was able to support,
then they crossed over to the Black Mountain,
even as far as the country of the glaciers,
where, hidden by an eternal wall of ice,
another people speaks another language.
In the Kernwald they built up the district Stanz,
and Altdorf in the valley of the Reuss –
but they did still remember where they came from:
in all the foreign races that since then
have settled in the middle of their country,

the men of Schwyz can pick each other out.
They recognise the heart, the blood, the race.
(*He holds his hand out left and right.*)
MAUER: Yes! We are of one heart, and of one blood.
ALL: (*Shaking hands.*) And of one race, and let us deal together!
STAUFFACHER: The other races bear a foreign yoke,
they have submitted to the conqueror.
Even inside our country's frontiers,
live many with divided loyalties,
passing their vassalage on to their children.
But we, the true race of the ancient Swiss,
have always kept our freedom for ourselves.
Never have we knelt to princes, but
freely chosen protection of the Emperor.
ROESSELMANN: The Empire's direct protection was our choice,
and so it stands in Kaiser Friedrich's charter.
STAUFFACHER: Even the freest of men must have a master:
there must be a supreme authority to judge
where the right may be found in any quarrel.
Our fathers, on this land, which they had conquered
from the old wilderness, gave this honour to
the Emperor, Lord of German lands and foreign,
and like the other free men of his Empire,
they promised loyal military service,
the only feudal duty of the free man,
to shield the Empire, by which they are shielded.
MELCHTAL: Anything else is sign of vassalage.
STAUFFACHER: When the Imperial call to arms was sounded,
they followed the flag and fought the Emperor's battles.
They rode in arms for him to Italy,
to set the crown of Rome upon his head.
At home they ruled themselves in all tranquillity
after old custom and the laws they'd made.
Only in capital crimes did the Emperor judge,
such judgment being delegated to
a powerful Count, not resident in the canton;
when it came to blood-guilt, he was called,
and, in the open air, aloud and clear,

he spoke the right, with neither fear nor favour.
    Where are the indications we are serfs?
    If anyone knows different, let him speak!
HOFE: No, all has been exactly as you said,
    we've never suffered rule of power here.
STAUFFACHER: And we refused the Kaiser our obedience,
    on his bending of the right to favour priests.
    For when the people of the monastery
    of Einsiedeln took possession of the mountain
    which we had grazed since our forefather's time,
    the abbot conjured up an ancient letter,
    bestowing on him this unclaimed desert –
    our own existence there had been ignored –
    at this we spoke: 'A contract gained by cunning.
    No emperor may bestow what's ours by right,
    and if the Empire should deny that right,
    we, in our mountains may deny the Empire.'
    That was how our fathers spoke! Should we
    suffer the new disgrace of yoke and shackles,
    and what no emperor dared offer us,
    must we accept that from his foreign subject?
    This land is something that we have created
    in the work of our own hands, the forest, which
    once was the savage habitat of bears,
    has been transformed into a place for men,
    killed is the dragon's brood, that rose,
    swollen with poison, from the marshy ground,
    the eternal veil of fog which hung there, grey,
    over this wilderness, we have torn down,
    blasted the mountain, over the precipice
    hewn a safe path for the wanderer's footsteps.
    We have been here for a thousand years
    and is a foreign bondman going to come
    to forge us shackles, and to offer us
    insult on our own soil? Is there no help
    that can be found against such grave compulsion?
    (*A great movement among those present.*)
    No, there are limits to the tyrant's power,

180

when the oppressed can nowhere find the right,
when the burden grows unbearable –
he will reach up to Heaven with assurance
and with the needful courage, grasp his rights,
that hang there like the very stars themselves,
inalienable, unchangeable, eternal –
Nature's primal condition's re-established
when Man is standing face to face with Man –
one last resource is left him when all others
have proved of no avail, he has his sword –
we may defend our highest good of all
against attack – we may defend our land,
defend our women and protect our children!

ALL: (*Beating their swords.*)
Defend our woman and protect our children!

ROESSELMANN: (*Stepping into the circle.*)
Before you draw your swords, consider carefully.
You might compose your discords with the Emperor
in peace. A word from you would bring those tyrants
who persecute you now, to fawn on you.
– accept what has been offered you so often,
give up the Empire, go with Austria!

MAUER: What did the priest say? In league with Austria?

BUEHEL: Don't listen to him!

WINKELRIED: Those words are a traitor's!
An enemy of our country!

REDING: Order, comrades!

SEWA: Homage to Austria, based on such dishonour!

FLUEE: Are we to let ourselves be bullied out
of what we have refused to yield to goodness?

MEIER: We would be slaves and would deserve to be!

MAUER: He who speaks of servitude to Austria
should forfeit all his rights to be a Swiss!
Chairman, I move that this should be the first
national law that we should pass.

MELCHTAL: So be it.
He who speaks of such accommodation
with Austria shall lose both rights and honours,

no patriot shall receive him at his hearth.

ALL: (*Raising their right hands.*)

We wish that to be law.

REDING: (*After a pause.*)   And law it is.

ROESSELMANN: That you are free, this law is proof enough.

Austria need no longer take by force,

what she cannot achieve by soft persuasion –

WEILER: Let us proceed with our agenda.

REDING: Comrades!

Are all the means of peace exhausted here?

Perhaps the King does not yet know, it cannot

truly be his will, the things we suffer.

Perhaps we should attempt this one last trial

to bring our grievance to his ear, before

our swords are out. Violence is always

terrible, even when the cause is just.

God only helps when men can help no longer.

STAUFFACHER: (*To Konrad HUNN.*)

Now it is your turn to report. So speak.

HUNN: I was at Rheinfeld, at the Emperor's palace,

to lodge complaints against the use of power

by the governors, and to demand the charter

of our ancient freedom which each new king

has always ratified. While I was there,

I found the representatives of many cities,

from lands of Swabia and along the Rhine,

all of them with parchments in their hands,

returning happily into their countries.

They consigned me, your messenger, to the councillors,

who then dismissed me with the empty comfort:

'His Majesty has no time on this occasion;

he will, however, keep your case in mind.'

And as I mournfully went through the halls,

I noticed Duke Johannes, weeping in a corner;

round him the noble lords of Wart and Tegerfeld,

who called to me and said: 'Shift for yourself,

and do not wait for justice from this King.

Has he not robbed his brother's eldest child,

deprived him of his just inheritance?
The Duke was begging for his mother's legacy.
He is now of age, and this is now the moment
when he should start to govern land and people.
What was the decision? The Emperor put
a garland on his head: the sign of youth.'

MAUER: You hear him? Right and Justice are not to be
expected of this emperor. Shift for yourselves!

REDING: There is no other way. Let us consider
the cleverest way to bring a happy end.

FUERST: (*Stepping into the circle.*)
We aim to abolish a detested force;
our ancient rights, that we inherited
from our forefathers, these we would preserve,
not indiscriminately grab the new.
Render to Caesar those things that are Caesar's;
he who has a master should obey him.

MEIER: I hold estates in fee from Austria.

FUERST: Then you are still in duty bound to them.

WEILER: I pay tax to the Counts of Rappersweil.

FUERST: Continue then to pay both rents and taxes.

ROESSELMANN: My oath is to Our Lady's Convent, in Zuerich.

FUERST: Give the convent those things that are the convent's.

STAUFFACHER: I hold no land in fee but from the Empire.

FUERST: What must be, let that be, but nothing more:
the Governors and all their underlings
we shall hunt out and then destroy their castles,
where possible without bloodshed. The Emperor
will see we act out of necessity
in setting aside respect for feudal duty;
but once he sees us staying in our limits,
political sense may mitigate his anger,
since any people must command respect,
who, sword in hand, will moderate themselves.

REDING: But let us hear now how we are to end it?
The enemy is the one to wield the weapons,
nor is he going to pick the path of peace.

STAUFFACHER: He will do so, when he sees us in arms.
    We shall surprise him before he can be ready.
MEIER: Easily said, but not so easily done.
    There are two castle strongholds in the land
    that shield the enemy and would be dangerous
    if the King should choose to march against us.
    Rossberg and Sarnen both must be subdued
    before a sword is drawn in the three cantons.
STAUFFACHER: Delay as long as that, we warn the enemy:
    there are too many sharers of the secret.
MEIER: In Unterwalden there will be no traitors.
ROESSELMANN: Excessive zeal, too, gives itself away.
FUERST: If we postpone, the fortress will be built
    in Altdorf, and the Governor inside it.
MEIER: You're thinking of yourselves.
KUONI: That is unjust.
MEIER: (*Flaring up.*) Unjust! Must we hear this from Uri?
REDING: By your oaths, peace!
MEIER: Oh, yes, when Schwyz and Uri
    make common cause, then we must hold our tongues.
REDING: I should denounce you to the council here
    for using violent words and thoughts against the peace!
    Are we not all identically committed?
WINKELRIED: If we delay till New Year's Day, the custom
    is for all feudal tenants to bring gifts
    to the Governors in the castle, ten or twelve
    men could meet there unsuspected, secretly
    carrying weapons that could quickly be
    attached to staves, since no one is allowed
    to bring a weapon within the castle walls.
    Meanwhile, in the forest, the main body of us
    wait for the others to control the gates
    and at a horn call, they will leave their ambush:
    the castle then, with not much work, is ours.
MELCHTAL: Then let me undertake to climb the Rossberg.
    There is a servant-girl who owes me much,
    her I can easily persuade, on my night visit
    to drop me a ladder; once up, I'll haul the others.

REDING: Is it the will of all, we should postpone?

(*The majority raise their hands.*)

STAUFFACHER: (*Counting the hands.*)

A majority of twenty against twelve!

FUERST: When, on the day agreed, the castles fall,

the beacons, from one mountain to another

will give the signal, and the general levy

will speedily be raised in every canton.

When the governors see the seriousness,

believe me, they will soon give up the struggle

and happily accept a peaceful convoy

out of the confines of our frontiers.

STAUFFACHER: The only one, I think, who'll make resistance

is Gessler, who, surrounded as he is

with men, will never leave the field without

bloodshed. Even driven from the field

he will still be a danger to the country.

It will be hard and dangerous to spare him.

BAUMGARTEN: If there is mortal danger, send me there.

My life was saved, I've Tell to thank for that.

Now I would gladly hazard it for my country.

My honour is preserved, my heart contented.

REDING: Time brings advice. Wait for it in patience.

Something must be entrusted to the moment.

But see, while we still keep our night-watch here,

the dawn already posts the watch of day

on the highest peaks – so come, let us break up,

before the daylight comes here to surprise us.

FUERST: The night ebbs slowly from the valleys. Never fear.

(*They have involuntarily removed their hats and gaze, in a general silence at the dawn.*)

ROESSELMANN: By this light, which we are first to greet

of all the peoples who, far down below,

draw their harsh breath amid the smoke of cities,

let us here swear the oath of our new league.

Oh, let us be a single band of brothers,

not to be parted by peril or distress.

(*All repeat the lines, raising three fingers.*)

Let us be free, as our forefathers were,
and rather die than live in slavery.
And let us put our trust in God Almighty,
no more to fear the might, the force of Men.
(*A general embrace.*)

STAUFFACHER:
Now each man go his way, back whence he came,
to friendship, comradeship and all that's dear:
the shepherd should prepare his flocks for winter,
and quietly win comrades for the league.
Whatever must be borne until that day,
let it be borne! Let the tyrant's bill
grow on, until one day it shall be paid
both in the general and particular.
Let each man tame his justified rage,
and save his vengeance for the general good,
for he does rob the general good who acts
just for himself in the particular.
(*As they disperse quietly to the three different sides, the orchestra
enters with splendid force, the empty stage remaining open for
a further while, showing the drama of the rising sun over the
icy mountains.*)

End of Act Two.

ACT THREE

Scene 1

Courtyard in front of TELL's house.
TELL is busy with an axe, HEDWIG with some domestic work.
WALTER and WILHELM are upstage, playing with a small crossbow.

WALTER: (*Singing.*) With his bow and arrows,
> The huntsman's on his way,
> Where the rock-path narrows,
> At the break of day.
In the air, by nature,
> The kite may be the king,
> In the rocks, the archer
> Is lord of everything.
His the farthest flight
> Of arrows through the skies,
> And he claims, by right,
> All that runs or flies.

The string's gone. Help me mend it, Father, please.
TELL: Not me. A proper bowman helps himself.
(*The boys withdraw.*)
HEDWIG: They've started learning shooting soon enough.
TELL: To be an expert, you can't start too soon.
HEDWIG: Ah, would to God they needn't learn at all!
TELL: They should learn everything. To get through life
with both defiance and defence, they must
be armed at all points.
HEDWIG: Who will ever find
peace at home? Nobody.
TELL: And nor can I:
Nature did not raise me for a shepherd,
but made me restless, chasing after movement;
the only way I can enjoy my life,
is by renewing daily such a contact.

187

HEDWIG: Without a single thought for all my terrors,
    which meanwhile grow and grow, waiting for you;
    it just fills me with horror, when I hear
    the peasants' stories of your reckless journeys.
    My heart goes cold each time we say goodbye,
    that you might never more come back to me.
    I see you in the savage, icy regions,
    lost, missing a jump from one rock to another,
    I see the chamois with a backward leap
    dragging you with it over the cliff, and how
    an avalanche could bury you, or how
    the treacherous glacier-snow might give and you
    be buried alive in some terrible crevasse –
    Death, in a hundred swiftly changing shapes,
    lies in the path of the rash Alpine hunter!
    It is a luckless, miserable profession
    which winds its breakneck way into the pit!
TELL: Whoever keeps his eyes well open, who
    is strong and agile and who trusts in God,
    can struggle out of any situation.
    No mountain frightens someone born on it.
    (*He has finished his work, and lays his tools by.*)
    That gate will hold another year and more.
    An axe at home will spare the carpenter. (*Takes his hat.*)
HEDWIG: Where are you going?
TELL: Altdorf, to see Father.
HEDWIG: You've nothing dangerous in mind? Now, have you?
TELL: What put that in your head?
HEDWIG: Something is afoot
    against the Governors – there was a meeting
    on the Ruetli, I know, and you were party to it.
TELL: I was not there – although I will admit
    I'll not desert the country, if it calls.
HEDWIG: And they would make you go where danger's worst,
    that will be your share of it, as usual.
TELL: Everyone is put where he's most use.
HEDWIG: You took the man from Unterwalden over
    the lake in the storm – it was a living wonder

that you escaped – had you no thought at all
for wife and child?

TELL: Dear wife, I thought of you,
that's why I saved the father, for his children.

HEDWIG: To take ship in that raging sea, that is
not trusting God, that is just tempting Him.

TELL: Who frets too much, will get but little done.

HEDWIG: Yes, good and helpful, ready to help all.
When you need help, though, you will find none.

TELL: Heaven forfend that I should ever need it.
(*Picks up his crossbow and arrows.*)

HEDWIG: Why do you take the crossbow? Leave it here.

TELL: Without a weapon, I feel I lack an arm.
(*The boys come back.*)

WALTER: Father, where are you going?

TELL: To Altdorf, son,
To see your Granddad. Want to come?

WALTER: Oh, yes.

HEDWIG: The Governor is at Altdorf. Stay away.

TELL: He leaves, today.

HEDWIG: Then let him first get clear.
Don't jog his memory, you know he hates us.

TELL: His mere dislike will not do much to hurt me,
I shall do nothing wrong, so fear no foe.

HEDWIG: It's those that do no wrong he hates the most.

TELL: Because he cannot get at them – I think
the gentleman will leave me on my own.

HEDWIG: How do you know that?

TELL: Not so long ago,
I was out hunting in the wildest parts
of the Schaechen valley, on tracks quite unfrequented,
and I was following a mountain path,
where I could never have turned aside,
since the rock-face was towering above me,
and down below me came the river's fearful roar.
(*The boys crowd up to him left and right, gazing up at him with
intense curiosity.*)
There towards me came the Governor.

He was alone with me, also alone,
just man to man, and next to us, the chasm.
And when he saw me, he knew me at once
for one he'd punished lately for scant cause.
Seeing me approaching with a weapon,
he lost all colour and his knees betrayed him,
I saw he might collapse at any minute,
against the rock-wall. And I felt some pity:
so I went to him, quietly saying, 'It is I',
but he could not produce a mortal sound
out of his mouth – no, with his hand, in silence,
he gestured, bidding me be on my way.
I did so, sending his retinue after him.

HEDWIG: He was afraid of you – and he will not
    forgive your seeing him betray his weakness.

TELL: So I avoid him, nor does he seek me out.

HEDWIG: Just do not go today. Can't you go hunting?

TELL: What are you saying?

HEDWIG: I'm frightened. Stay away.

TELL: How can you be so anxious, for no reason?

HEDWIG: Because there is no reason – Tell, stay here.

TELL: Dearest wife, I promised I would come.

HEDWIG: Then if you must, you must – leave me the boy.

WALTER: No, Mother, no. I'm going with my father.

HEDWIG: So, you are leaving your mother all alone?

WALTER: I'll bring a present for you, back from Granddad.
    (*Goes out with his father.*)

WILHELM: Mother, I'll stay with you!

HEDWIG (*Embracing him.*)   Oh, yes, you are
    my good child, you are all that's left me!
    (*She goes to the courtyard gate and follows the travellers with
    her eyes for a long while.*)

Scene 2

A closed-in forest region. Streams fall in spray down the rocks.

BERTA: (*In hunting costume, followed by RUDENZ.*)
  He's following me.
RUDENZ: (*Entering quickly.*)
  Madame, at last I find you on your own,
  locked in by abysses on every side,
  I have at least no fear of witnesses,
  now I can shake my heart free from this silence –
BERTA: You're sure the huntsmen are not following us?
RUDENZ: The hunt's a long way off – it's now or never!
  I have to seize the moment when I can –
  I have to know the nature of my fate,
  even if it takes you from me forever.
  Oh, do not arm the bounty of your glance,
  with such a mighty darkness – who am I
  to show you evidence of such presumption?
  I am not yet sought out by Fame, I may
  not stand in line for you with noble knights,
  whose splendid victories vie for your hand.
  I only have a faithful, loving heart –
BERTA: (*Serious, and firm.*)
  You dare to speak of love and faithfulness,
  who faithlessly betrayed his own first duty?
RUDENZ: Am I hearing this reproach from you?
  Whom have I sought on every side but you?
BERTA: And did you think to find me on the side
  of treachery? I'd rather give my hand
  to Gessler, the oppressor himself, than to
  such a degenerate son of Switzerland
  who lets himself be made the oppressor's tool.
RUDENZ: Oh God, what must I hear?
BERTA: What? What lies
  nearer the good man than his family?
  No duty closer to a noble heart
  than, as defender of the innocent,
  to champion the rights of the oppressed.

My soul bleeds for your people, and I suffer
with them, since I must love them, when they are
so unpretentious yet so full of strength.
With all my heart, I am attracted to them,
and every day I find more to admire.
But you, by birth and honour their protector,
who has deserted them, who faithlessly
went over to the enemy, who has forged
chains for his country, you are the one who has
mortified me and grieved me. I must
subdue my heart, if I am not to hate you.

RUDENZ: Do I not want the best for all my people?
Assuring it, beneath the mighty sceptre
of Austria, peace –

BERTA: It's slavery you prepare!
You would drive Liberty out of every house
which is still yours upon the face of the earth.
The common people know their fortune better,
they are not taken in by any sham,
and they have thrown the net about your head.

RUDENZ: Berta! How you hate me, and despise me.

BERTA: Better for me, much better if I did.
To see the man despised, and rightly so,
whom one would so much sooner love –

RUDENZ: Oh, Berta!
You show me all of Heaven that I've known,
yet in that moment, I am overthrown.

BERTA: No no, nobility is not quite dead
in you! It only sleeps, and I shall wake it.
You have to use much violence on yourself
to mortify your native virtue, but
take courage, it is stronger far than you:
despite yourself, you are still good and noble.

RUDENZ: Then you have faith in me? Berta, your love
allows me to be everything, or become it!

BERTA: Then be what Nature framed you for and fill
the place she chose for you. Stand by your country
and by your people – fight for your holy right!

RUDENZ: How can I achieve you, or possess you,
     if I oppose the power of the Emperor?
     And is it not the might of your relations
     that tyrannously allocates your hand?
BERTA: All my estates lie this side of the frontier,
     so if the Swiss are free, then so am I.
RUDENZ: Berta! What a look you are giving me!
BERTA: Do not hope to win me by Austria's favour;
     they too are stretching out their greedy hands
     for my inheritance to add to theirs.
     The territorial greed which threatens you
     with loss of freedom, menaces me too!
     I am picked out to be a victim here,
     perhaps to pay off a court favourite –
     but where false witness and intriguers sit,
     at the Emperor's court I must appear,
     where I await those hated marriage-chains!
     To free me, only love – your love – remains!
RUDENZ: And could you then decide to settle here,
     and give yourself to me, here, in my country?
     O Berta, what has all my wandering
     been but a journey to be by your side?
     All that I looked for on the path of Fame,
     all my ambition was my love for you.
     Could you but withdraw with me into
     this quiet valley, and give up the world –
     oh, then my struggle would have found its mark!
     The current of this wild, tumultuous world
     would beat upon the safe shore of these mountains –
     I have no further transient desire
     to send into the vastnesses of Life –
     then let the rocks that here, and now, surround us
     extend these strong, impenetrable walls,
     let only this shut-in but happy valley,
     be open to the heavens and illumined!
BERTA: Now you are everything my heart foresaw
     and dreamed of! And my faith was not deceived!

RUDENZ: Farewell to that vain madness that befooled me!
I'll find my happiness in my own land!
Here, where I passed my happy boyhood years;
here, where a thousand joys surrounded me;
here, where the springs and trees lived just for me;
here, in my Fatherland, you will be mine!
Yes, I have always loved it, and I feel
I needed it in every happiness.
BERTA: Where are the islands of the blessèd found
if not here, in the land of innocence?
Here, where old Loyalty has always dwelt,
where Falsity finds nowhere to alight;
where envy does not muddy our good fortune,
and where the hours fly past us, ever bright:
there I can see you in your full man's worth,
First of your peers and free, on your own ground,
with purer, freer homage come to birth,
like a great king, in his great empire's round.
RUDENZ: As I see you, you crown of womankind,
in all your woman's charm and occupation,
within my house you have a heaven designed.
As Spring spreads flowers with easy ostentation,
with Grace you ornament and bless my days,
reviving all around in a thousand ways!
BERTA: You see, my dearest friend, why I was downcast
to see you wreck, and by yourself, your chance
of highest happiness – How would I be
if I was forced to follow the proud knight,
oppressor of his country, to his dark tower?
There is no fortress here. No walls divide me
from a people I can bring some happiness.
RUDENZ: But how to save myself? Undo the noose
my own futility put round my neck?
BERTA: Tear it in two! Decide it like a man!
Whatever comes of it – stand by your people!
That is what you were born to.
(*Hunting horns in the distance.*)   There is the hunt.
They're coming – Go, we have to separate –

Fight for your country. It's fighting for your love!
There is one enemy, before whom we all tremble,
there is one liberty, that will free us all!
(*They go out.*)

Scene 3

*A square in Altdorf. In the foreground there are trees, in the
background the hat on a pole. The stage is cut off by a view of
the Bannberg, behind which a snowy peak can be seen.
FRIESSHARDT and LEUTHOLD are on guard.*

FRIESSHARDT: A waste of time, this watch. Nobody's going
　　to come this way to make his bow to a hat.
　　Other days it'd be a fairground here:
　　today the whole place is a desert waste,
　　ever since the scarecrow's lid was up there.
LEUTHOLD: Only the riff-raff shows its face, and forces us
　　to see their dirty caps, more than we'd want.
　　The quality prefers to take the long way round
　　rather than bow and curtsy to the hat.
FRIESSHARDT: They have to go across this square when they
　　come from the Town Hall in the lunch hour, when
　　I thought we'd make a good catch, since nobody
　　would ever think of bowing to the hat.
　　Then Roesselmann, the priest, was coming
　　straight from a sickbed, noticed it and stood,
　　wafer in hand, right in front of the pole.
　　The sexton had to ring his little bell,
　　and all of us fell on our knees, me too,
　　bowed to the sacrament, and not the hat.
LEUTHOLD: Listen, friend, I'm getting the impression
　　that we are being made the guys in this.
　　On sentry duty for an empty hat,
　　is not a job to give a cavalryman.
　　Any regular soldier would despise us.
　　To have to bow and scrape for an empty hat,
　　I mean, for God's sake! What a stupid order!

FRIESSHARDT: What is so bad about an empty hat?
   You bow before a mort of empty heads.
   (*HILDEGARD, MECHTHILD and ELSBET enter with their*
   children and stand round the pole.)
LEUTHOLD: And you're a servile bit of work, and all,
   you'd like to see the best of us come to grief.
   Whoever wants to just walk past the hat,
   they're welcome. I shall look the other way.
MECHTHILD:
   There hangs the Governor – show respect, you kids.
ELSBET: Why can't he go, and leave his hat behind?
   Things here would not get any worse for that!
FRIESSHARDT: Be off with you, go on! Damned womenfolk!
   Who cares for you ? Why don't you send your men,
   if you're so brave to disobey an order?
   (*The women go. Enter TELL upstage, carrying his crossbow,*
   leading WALTHER by the hand. They walk on past the hat
   without paying any attention to it.)
WALTHER: (*Pointing to the Bannberg.*)
   Father, is it true that up there on the mountain,
   the trees shed blood when someone puts a gash
   in with an axe?
TELL: Who told you that, son?
WALTHER: Shepherds –
   they said the trees were under the protection
   of witchcraft, and that anyone who hurt them,
   a hand would grow and follow to the grave.
TELL: They are protected, that much is the truth.
   You see the snows up there, the two high peaks
   that rise until they're lost up in the sky?
WALTHER: The glaciers that thunder in the night
   when they are going to send an avalanche?
TELL: That's right, and avalanches would have brought
   the town of Altdorf to destruction with
   their weight. The trees up there serve as a barrier.
WALTHER: (*After a little thought.*)
   Are there countries, then, that don't have mountains?

TELL: When you travel down from our high places,
    keep going downwards, following the rivers:
    you'll come at last to a wide, flat countryside,
    where water does not flow in noisy streams,
    but rivers wind by, peacefully and gently;
    the harvest ripens there in long, fair, fields,
    and you can see the country like a garden.
WALTHER: Hey, Father, why do we not quickly go
    down to this country, if it is so good,
    and leave the troubles that we have up here?
TELL: The land is fair and kind, just like the sky,
    but those who build on it, they do not have
    the good of what they plant.
WALTHER: Why? Do they not
    live free, like you, on land which is their own?
TELL: The fields belong to the bishops and the King.
WALTHER: Then people can go hunting in the forests.
TELL: The nobles are the owners of the game.
WALTHER: But they can still go fishing in the river?
TELL: The salt, the sea, the rivers – all the King's.
WALTHER: Who is this King, then, they're all so afraid of?
TELL: He is the one man who protects and feeds them.
WALTHER: Are they not brave enough to feed themselves?
TELL: Neighbours do not trust each other there.
WALTHER: Father, the open land would shut me in,
    I'd rather live among the avalanches.
TELL: You're right, son, it is better far to have
    the glaciers at your back than wicked people.
    (*They are making as if to go out.*)
WALTHER: Hey, father, look, a hat up on a pole.
TELL: What's that to do with us? Come on, let's go.
    (*Just as they are going, FRIESSHARDT steps in the way, pike
    at the ready.*)
FRIESSHARDT:
    Halt in the name of the Emperor! Halt and stand!
TELL: (*Grabbing the pike.*)
    What do you want? Why have you made me stop?
FRIESSHARDT: You disobeyed an order. Come with us.

LEUTHOLD: You failed to show the hat the due respect.

TELL: Let me be on my way, friend.

FRIESSHARDT: Yes, to prison!

WALTHER: Father in prison? (*Shouting off.*)

                                    Help there, help, good people,
they're taking him to prison!

(*ROESSELMANN the priest, and the sexton PETERMANN
enter, with three others.*)

PETERMANN: What's all this?

ROESSELMANN: Why have you laid hands upon this man?

FRIESSHARDT: An enemy of the Emperor and a traitor.

TELL: (*Grabbing him violently.*)

Me a traitor!

ROESSELMANN: There you are quite wrong, friend.
That is Tell, a man of honour and
a highly respected citizen.

(*Seeing WALTER FUERST, WALTHER runs over to him.*)

WALTHER: Grandfather, help, they're taking Father away!

FRIESSHARDT: Come on, to prison!

FUERST: (*Hurrying over.*)   I'll stand surety!
Halt! – in God's name, Tell, what's happening?

(*MELCHTAL and STAUFFACHER enter.*)

FRIESSHARDT:

He showed contempt for the Governor's authority
And wouldn't recognise it either.

STAUFFACHER: Do you tell me
that Tell did such a thing?

MELCHTAL: You're lying, boy.

LEUTHOLD: He failed to show the hat the due respect.

FUERST: And so he goes to prison? Friend, a word.
Just take my guarantee and let him go.

FRIESSHARDT: You guarantee yourself while you're about it!
We're only doing our duty – take him away!

MELCHTAL: (*To the people.*)

No! That is arrant violence! Are we going
to stand for that, before our very eyes?

SEXTON: We are the stronger. Friends, do not accept it,
remember that we have support behind us!

FRIESSHARDT: Who is it defies the Governor's orders?

THREE MEN: (*Running in.*)

    We'll help you. What's the matter? Knock 'em down.

    (*HILDEGARD, MECHTHILD and ELSBET come back in.*)

TELL: I can help myself. Go now, good people,

    d'you think if I should choose to use my strength

    that I should be afraid of all their weapons?

MELCHTAL: (*To FRIESSHARDT.*)

    Come on then, dare to try and take him from us!

FUERST / STAUFFACHER:

    Hold off now! Quiet!

FRIESSHARDT: (*Screaming.*) Riot and Sedition!

    (*Hunting horns are heard.*)

WOMEN: The Governor's coming!

FRIESSHARDT: (*Raising his voice.*) Mutiny! Revolution!

STAUFFACHER:

    Scream till you burst, you rogue!

ROESSELMANN / MELCHTAL: Will you be quiet!

FRIESSHARDT: (*Louder still.*)

    Help me, help the guardians of the Law!

FUERST: The Governor! Ah! What will happen now?

    (*Enter GESSLER on horseback, a falcon on his wrist, Rudolf der HARRAS, BERTA and RUDENZ, with a considerable train of ARMED MEN, who form a circle of pikes around the whole scene.*)

HARRAS: Room there! Room for the Governor!

GESSLER: Separate them!

    What are these people doing? Who called for help?

    (*Total silence.*)

    Who was it ? I want to know.

    (*To FRIESSHARDT.*)   You there, forward.

    Who are you and why do you hold that man?

    (*Gives the falcon to a servant.*)

FRIESSHARDT: Your Honour, Sir, I am your man-at-arms,

    duly appointed guardian of the hat.

    I saw this man, and duly apprehended,

    for neglecting his respect due to the hat.

    I wanted to arrest him, as you ordered,

and now the people want to set him free.

GESSLER: (*After a pause.*)

Do you despise your emperor so much,
and me, Tell, who here gives orders in his stead,
that you deny the honour due the hat,
which I put there for testing your obedience?
Your bad intent betrays itself to me.

TELL: Pardon me, Your Honour. Lack of thought
and not contempt brought this about.
If it were not, my name would not be Tell.
Forgive me, Sire, it will not be repeated.

GESSLER: You are a master with the crossbow, Tell,
they say, you are a match for any bowman?

WALTHER: That's true, sir, he can shoot an apple off
the tree for you, and at a hundred paces.

GESSLER: Is this your boy, Tell?

TELL: Yes, it is, Your Honour.

GESSLER: Do you have more children?

TELL: Two boys, Sire.

GESSLER: And which one is it that you love the most?

TELL: Sire, I love both my children equally.

GESSLER: Then, Tell, since you can shoot an apple
off of the tree, and at a hundred paces,
you must give me a demonstration of
your skill – pick up your crossbow – there it is
close to hand – and then prepare yourself
to shoot an apple off this young man's head –
only I must advise you, take good aim
to see you hit the apple at first shot,
since, if you miss, your own head will be forfeit.
(*All show signs of horror.*)

TELL: My Lord, – this monstrous thing you're asking me
to do – from my boy's head that I – oh no,
my good Lord, no, that cannot be your meaning –
may God forbid – you cannot seriously
want such a thing – to ask it of a father!

GESSLER: You will shoot the apple off the head
of the boy – I want it and I shall have it.

TELL: With my crossbow I am then to take aim
  at the head of my own child – I'd rather die!
GESSLER: You shoot or die together with your boy.
TELL: I am to be the murderer of my child!
  My Lord, you have no children – cannot know
  the springs of feeling in a father's heart.
GESSLER: Ach, Tell, you're suddenly a realist!
  They told me you were rather a romantic,
  keeping apart from other people's ways.
  You love the unusual – which is the reason
  I pick a deed of daring just for you.
  Another man might hesitate – but you
  shut your eyes tight and tackle it with courage.
BERTA: My good Lord, do not joke with these poor people,
  staring at you, pale and trembling – they
  are little used to hearing jokes from you.
GESSLER: Who told you I was joking?
  (*Reaching for a branch over his head.*)   Here! an apple!
  Now, make some room there – let him take his distance,
  that is the rule – I give him eighty paces –
  no more, no less – he was the one that boasted
  that he could hit his man at a hundred –
  well, marksman, shoot now, do not miss the target.
HARRAS: God, this is serious. Down, boy, on your knees,
  right now, and beg the Governor for your life.
FUERST: (*Aside to MELCHTAL, who can barely conceal his
  impatience.*) Control yourself, I beg you, keep your head.
BERTA: (*To GESSLER.*)
  Oh, let that be enough. It is inhuman
  to play with a father's feelings in this way.
  When this poor man has forfeited his life,
  and for so slight a fault, by God, he would
  by now have suffered death, and ten times over.
  Let him go back unharmed, back to his house,
  he knows you now: this meeting will be one
  he will remember with his grandchildren.
GESSLER: Open the lane – Well, what are you waiting for?
  Your life is forfeit, I could kill you now,

yet here I am merciful enough to place
your destiny in your own skilled hand. It is
ungrateful to resent too harsh a sentence,
when one is made the master of his fate.
You pride yourself on sharpness of your eye.
Here is a chance then, Marksman, to display it.
The target's worthy and the prize is great!
Anyone can hit the bull's eye in
a target! But what I would call a master
is the man, sure of his skill on all occasions,
whose heart does not distract his hand or eye.

FUERST: (*Throwing himself at GESSLER's feet.*)
Lord Governor, we recognise your rank,
only let Mercy season Justice. Take
half of what I have, no, take it all,
but spare a father from this dreadful trial!

WALTHER: Grandfather, do not kneel to that false man!
Tell me where I must stand. I'm not afraid.
Father can hit a bird when it's in flight,
he won't miss when he's shooting at my heart.

STAUFFACHER: Are you not moved by this child's innocence?

ROESSELMANN: Remember, there's a God in Heaven above you,
to whom you must account for all your actions.

GESSLER: Tie the boy to that tree!

WALTHER: What? Tie me, no!
I do not want to be. I will hold still.
I'll be just like a lamb, not even breathe.
But if you tie me, I can't do it then,
I'd have to struggle against the ropes.

HARRAS: Then let
Them bind your eyes, boy.

WALTHER: Why my eyes?
You think I'm frightened by an arrow from
my father's hand? I will stand ready for it,
not moving by so much as a single eyelash.
Now, father, show them what a shot you are!
He won't believe it, and he wants to ruin us,
so spite the bloody tyrant, shoot and hit.

(*He goes to the tree. They put the apple on his head.*)

MELCHTAL: (*To the COUNTRYMEN.*)

What? Shall this crime take place before our eyes?

What did we take our oaths on? What did we swear?

STAUFFACHER: It is no use. We have no weapons here,

and see the forest of lances that surrounds us!

MELCHTAL: Oh, why did we not act immediately?

God forgive those who voted for delay!

GESSLER: (*To TELL.*) To work! Weapons should not be idly worn.

Carrying a lethal weapon is a danger:

the arrow can rebound against the bowman.

And this proud right, that every peasant claims,

is an insult to the highest in the land.

None should go armed, except he who gives orders.

It pleases you to carry bow and arrows;

all well and good, but I pick out the target.

TELL: (*Winds up the crossbow and sets the quarrel in place.*)

Open the lane there! Room!

STAUFFACHER:

What, Tell? You mean to – Never – you are trembling,

your hand's not steady, and your knees are shaking –

TELL: (*Letting the crossbow sink.*)

It's swimming before my eyes.

WOMEN: Dear God in Heaven!

TELL: (*To GESSLER.*)

Absolve me from the shot. Here is my heart.

(*Exposes his chest.*)

Summon your pikemen. Have them strike me down.

GESSLER: I do not want your life: I want that shot.

You can do anything, Tell, nothing daunts you,

you work a tiller as you use a bow,

you fear no storm, if you are saving someone,

now, Saviour, save yourself – you save it all!

(*TELL stands in a terrible struggle. His hands twitch, his eyes
are fixed now on GESSLER, now up to Heaven. Suddenly he
reaches into his quiver, pulls out a second bolt and puts it into
his jacket. GESSLER observes all these movements.*)

WALTHER: (*Under the tree.*)
  Shoot, Father, shoot. I'm not afraid.
TELL: Must be!
  (*Pulls himself together and takes aim.*)
RUDENZ: (*Who has stood the whole time in the most violent
  suspense, now steps forward.*)
  My lord, you will not press this matter any further,
  you will not – it has only been a trial –
  the point is made – impelling things too far
  weakens the strength of your most wise intent.
  Stretch the bow too tight and it will break.
GESSLER: Be quiet until you're spoken to.
RUDENZ: I will speak!
  And I may. The Emperor's honour I hold sacred,
  but such misrule can only waken hatred:
  it is not, I maintain, the Imperial will.
  Such cruelty my people don't deserve,
  nor have you the authority to exercise it.
GESSLER: Ha, we are getting bolder!
RUDENZ: I've kept silence
  about those heavy actions I have witnessed;
  I shut my eyes, and forced my sickened heart
  into my breast. But any further silence
  would betray both my country and my King.
BERTA: (*Throwing herself between RUDENZ and GESSLER.*)
  Oh, God, you'll only anger him the more.
RUDENZ: My people I abandoned, and denied
  my family, destroyed all bonds of nature,
  in order to connect myself to you –
  I thought that I was furthering the good,
  since I was strengthening the Emperor's power.
  The scales have fallen from my eyes – with horror
  I see myself at the edge of an abyss –
  my balanced judgment you have led astray,
  seduced an honest heart – I was prepared,
  with best intentions, to destroy my people.
GESSLER: Insolence! Is that how you speak to your lord?

RUDENZ: The Emperor is my lord, not you – I was
    born as free a man as you, and I
    esteem myself your equal in all matters
    of knightly honour. Did you not stand there
    in the Emperor's name, which I do honour to,
    even when disgrace is brought upon it,
    I would throw down my glove, and you would have
    to give me answer, as the knightly custom
    demands – yes, call your troopers, do – but I am not
    defenceless, like these men – (*Pointing to the TOWNSPEOPLE.*)
                                    I wear a sword,
    And anyone who comes –
STAUFFACHER: The apple's hit!
    (*While everyone was turned towards the other side, and BERTA
    had thrown herself between RUDENZ and GESSLER, TELL
    had fired off the arrow.*)
ROESSELMANN: The boy's alive!
VARIOUS VOICES: The apple! Look! It's hit!
    (*FUERST sways and threatens to collapse. BERTA holds
    him up.*)
GESSLER: (*Astonished.*)
    You mean he really fired? The man is mad!
BERTA: The boy's alive! Father, come to yourself!
WALTHER: (*Scurrying forward with the apple.*)
    Father, the apple's here – I always knew
    you wouldn't do anything to hurt me.
    (*TELL stands bent forward, as if he were going to follow the
    path of the arrow – the crossbow sinks from his hand – as he sees
    the boy coming towards him, he hurries to him with outstretched
    arms and holds him up to his heart with violent ardour, in which
    position he sinks senseless to the ground. Everyone stands still,
    deeply moved.*).
BERTA: Merciful Heaven!
FUERST: (*To father and son.*) Children! Oh, my children!
STAUFFACHER: May the Lord be praised!
LEUTHOLD: That was a shot!
    They'll talk about that shot till I don't know when.

HARRAS: They'll talk about the marksman Tell, until
the mountains there no longer stand their ground.
(*Hands GESSLER the apple.*)

GESSLER: By God, the apple, shot right through the middle!
A master-shot, I must congratulate him.

ROESSELMANN: The shot was good, but woe then to the man
who drove him to it; he was tempting God.

STAUFFACHER: Wake up, Tell, stand up, you acted bravely,
now you are free to go back to your home.

ROESSELMANN:
Come, come, and bring the mother back her son.
(*They are about to take him away.*)

GESSLER: Tell, listen!

TELL: (*Coming back.*) What are your orders, Sir?

GESSLER: You took
a second quarrel out and hid it – yes,
you did, I saw you – what did you mean by that?

TELL: Sire, it's a habit all the marksmen have.

GESSLER: No, Tell, that answer I cannot accept,
there must have been another meaning to it.
So let me have the truth now, pure and simple:
be it what it may, I guarantee your life.
Why the second arrow?

TELL: Very well,
My Lord, since you have guaranteed my life,
then I shall give you up the honest truth.
(*He produces the second arrow from his jacket, and gives
GESSLER a fearsome look.*)
This second arrow I'd have shot at – you,
if I had hit my dearest child, and you,
let me assure you, I would not have missed.

GESSLER: Well, Tell! I guaranteed your life. I gave
my word – as I'm a gentleman, I'll not break it –
however, since I recognise your rank ill-will,
I'm going to have you taken and shut up,
where neither sun nor moon will shine on you,
I shall, at least, be safe then from your arrows.
lay hold on him, men, bind him!

(*TELL is tied up.*)

STAUFFACHER: What, my Lord?

Is this a way for dealing with a man

clearly in the keeping of God's hand?

GESSLER: Then let us see if He will save him twice.

Have him brought on my ship! I'll come at once,

and personally see him conveyed to Kuessnacht.

ROESSELMANN:

You mean to take him from the canton as a prisoner?

TOWNSPEOPLE: You cannot do that, nor can the Emperor,

it is in contradiction to our charters.

GESSLER: Where are these charters, now? Has the Emperor

confirmed them? No, the Emperor has not

confirmed them. That is a favour which is granted

only on condition of obedience.

You are all rebels against the Emperor's Law,

harbouring insolent feelings of revolt.

I know you all – and I see through you all –

I take this man out of the midst of you,

but all of you are sharers in his guilt.

Be clever, and learn silence and obedience.

(*He goes out, followed by BERTA, RUDENZ, HARRAS and the
soldiers. FRIESSHARDT and LEUTHOLD stay behind.*)

FUERST: It is all over, he is determined to

destroy me and my house and family!

STAUFFACHER: (*To TELL.*)

Why did you have to rouse his anger, Tell?

TELL: He who can feel my pain, let him keep calm!

STAUFFACHER: Now all is over. We are bound and chained

along with you.

TOWNSPEOPLE: (*Surrounding TELL.*)

                    With you, our last hope's gone!

LEUTHOLD: (*Approaching.*)

Tell, beg your pardon – must obey my orders.

TELL: Goodbye!

WALTHER: (*Clinging to him in agony.*)

                    Oh, Father! Dearest father, please!

TELL: (*Raising his arms to Heaven.*)

    Your father is up there! So call him there!!

STAUFFACHER: Tell, should I not say anything to your wife?

TELL: (*Picks the boy up and holds him fervently to his heart.*)

    The boy has not been harmed, and God will help me.

    (*Tears himself loose and follows the men-at-arms.*)

    End of Act Three.

ACT FOUR

Scene 1

East bank of the lake of Lucerne. The strangely formed cliffs to the West border the view. The lake is violently surging and roaring, in between flashes of lightning and claps of thunder.

Kunz von GERSAU, RUODI the fisherman and JENNI his boy.

GERSAU: Saw it with my own eyes, you must believe it,
    everything happened just as I have said.

RUODI: Tell, taken as a prisoner to Kussnacht.
    The best man in the country, and the bravest,
    whenever a blow had to be struck for Freedom.

GERSAU: The Governor himself brought him across
    the lake; they were preparing to embark
    as I came up from Flueelen, though the storm
    that's brewing still, and which caused me too
    to make a landing here, and in a hurry,
    may well have interfered with their departure.

RUODI: Tell in fetters, and the Governor's prisoner!
    You can be sure he'll bury him deep enough,
    so that he'll never see the light of day!
    Since he'll have need to fear the just revenge
    of a free man whom he's injured and insulted.

GERSAU: The noble Herr von Attinghausen, too,
    leader of our community, they say, is dying.

RUODI: Then the last anchor of our hopes is gone!
    He was the only one who'd raise his voice,
    to speak in favour of the people's rights!

GERSAU: The storm is getting worse, I'll say farewell.
    I'll shelter in the village. There's no thought
    of casting off again on such a day. (*Exit.*)

RUODI: Tell taken prisoner and the Freiherr dead!
    Tyranny, now dare to show your face,
    throw shame aside. The mouth that spoke the truth
    is dumb, the eye that saw the truth is blind,
    the arm that was to save, is bound in chains.

JENNI: It's coming on to hail. Take shelter, Father.
It isn't good to be out in the open.
RUODI: Blow, blow, you winds, and lightnings, send down fire,
clouds, burst and pour down all the rivers of Heaven
to drown the land! Destroy now, in the seed,
the generations all as yet unborn!
You, the wild elements, take the mastery!
You bears, come now, you ancient wolves,
out of the deserts now, the land belongs to you!
For who would live there gladly without freedom?
JENNI: Listen! The pit is roaring, and the whirlpool,
the gulf has never raged like this before!
RUODI: To aim an arrow at his own child's head,
was never a father made to do before.
Nature demands redress, so angered is she
by an unnatural deed – I shouldn't wonder
to see the rocks bow low across the lake,
to see the icy peaks that never thawed
since the first day of their creation,
melting from their high summits, and the mountains
crumbling, while the precipices fall,
bringing a second deluge onto all
the habitations of the human race!
(*Bells are heard ringing.*)
JENNI: Listen! They're ringing on the mountain.
Somebody must have seen a ship in danger,
and rings the bells to tell us all to pray.
(*Steps up higher.*)
RUODI: Pity the craft that's going anywhere,
this is no cradle to be rocked in.
Tiller and tillerman alike are useless now.
The storm is master. Men are tennis-balls
for wind and waves to play at – far and wide
no bay in which they can find friendly shelter!
Offering no handhold, inhospitably,
the rocks stare back at him, and offer him
nothing but their stony, plunging breasts.
JENNI: (*Pointing off left.*) Father, a ship. It's coming from Flueelen.

RUODI: God help the poor folk on board her!
    If the storm takes hold here in the narrows,
    then it will rage in fury like a beast,
    beating against the iron bars of a cage;
    a harbour he will never find, surrounded
    by rocks that block the pass up to the sky.
    (*He climbs up higher.*)
JENNI: It is the Governor's boat, from Uri, Father,
    I can see the red roof and the pennant on it.
RUODI: Justice of God! The Governor himself
    is travelling on it – carrying his crimes
    along with him! But the arm of vengeance
    has quickly found him out. Now he will know
    there is a higher master over him:
    these waves will not retreat at his command,
    these rocks will not do reverence to
    his hat – come, boy, come on and do not pray,
    the Judge above will need no help from you!
JENNI: Not praying for the Governor. It's for Tell,
    if he is with the Governor on the ship.
RUODI: Unreason of unseeing elements!
    To hit one guilty man, why do you have
    to carry off the whole ship and the crew?
JENNI: Look, look, they had just cleared the Buggisgrat,
    when the storm's power drove them back again,
    from the Teufelsmuenster to the Axenberg.
    I can't see any more.
RUODI: There is the Hakmesser
    sticking out from the Axenberg, where many
    good ships have foundered. If they're not cleverly
    steered, they will get broken on the Fluh
    which sinks down like a cliff into the deep.
    They will need a good steersman on board. Tell
    could do it, but he's bound hand and foot.
    (*TELL enters, with his crossbow. He advances rapidly, looks
    around him with astonishment, showing the strongest emotion.
    When he has got to the middle of the stage, he throws himself
    down, hands to the earth and then spread out to the skies.*)

JENNI: (*Noticing him.*)

　　Look, Father, who's the man that's kneeling there?

RUODI: He's grasping at the earth with both his hands,

　　he seems to be exhausted.

JENNI: (*Coming forwards.*)

　　What is this? Father, Father, come and look!

RUODI: (*Approaching.*)

　　Who is it? – God in Heaven! What? It's Tell!

　　How did you get here? Tell us!

JENNI:　　　　　　　　　　　　　Weren't you

　　a prisoner, tied up, on the ship? And weren't they…

RUODI: Did they not take you off to Kuessnacht, then?

TELL: (*Stands.*) I am free.

RUODI:　　　　　　　　　Free? That's a miracle, though!

JENNI: Where have you come from?

TELL:　　　　　　　　　　　　　Out of the ship there.

RUODI:　　　　　　　　　　　　　　　　　　　What?

JENNI: Where is the Governor?

TELL:　　　　　　　　　　　　Drifting on the waves.

RUODI: Is that possible? But you? How did you get here?

　　Escaping both your shackles and the storm?

TELL: God's merciful providence – listen to me.

RUODI: Oh, tell us, tell us!

TELL:　　　　　　　　　　Everything that happened

　　in Altdorf you have heard?

RUODI:　　　　　　　　　　I know it all, but tell us.

TELL: How the Governor took me prisoner and bound me,

　　meaning to take me to his keep at Kuessnacht.

RUODI: And taking ship with you at Flueelen!

　　We know all that, but say how you escaped!

TELL: I lay there in the ship's hold, tightly bound,

　　abandoned and defenceless – without hope

　　of ever seeing daylight any more,

　　nor the dear faces of my wife and children,

　　I looked over the desert of the waters –

RUODI: Poor fellow!

TELL:　　　　　　　So we travelled on: the Governor,

　　Rudolf the Horse-Master, and the men-at-arms.

My crossbow and my quiver were, however,
lying in the stern close to the steersman.
Then, as we drew alongside the small Axen,
God disposed that such a murderous blast
suddenly blew from the chasm of the Gotthard,
that all the oarsmen felt their hearts turn over,
and faced a miserable death by drowning.
Just at this point I heard a servant say,
turning towards the Governor: 'My Lord,
you see the danger we and you are in,
we are all standing on the brink of death –
the steersmen have no notion what do,
for fear and inexperience in sailing.
However, there is that Tell can sail a ship:
how if we used his skill in this emergency?'
The Governor said to me: 'Tell, if you think
you can help us through this storm, I'd be prepared
to disengage your shackles.' I replied:
'Sire, with God's aid, I'll venture it and help
to take us through.' So I was freed, and stood
at the wheel, and steered my best, but took a glance
sideways to where my quiver lay, and another
closely watching the bank to see if there
could be an opportunity to jump ashore.
And when I saw a flat, projecting rock
jutting into the sea –

RUODI: I know it, at
the bigger Axen's foot, but can't believe
it could be reached by jumping from a boat –

TELL: I shouted to the men to do their bravest
till we had come up level with the rock,
that, I said, would bring us past the worst –
and when, by rowing strongly, we came up
with the rock, I said a prayer to God, and pressed
with every ounce of strength left in my body
the boat's stern off the rockface, snatched my bow
and swung myself onto the platform, giving
a powerful kick behind me to the boat,

which took it to the current of the water,
where it could take its chance with God's good will.
So I came here, saved, both from the power
of the weather and the worser power of men.

TELL: Tell, Tell, the Lord has worked a miracle
for you, I hardly can believe it yet –
but tell me, where d'you think you're going now?
There is no safety for you, if the Governor
manages to escape this storm alive.

TELL: I heard him say, while I was lying bound,
he meant to land at Brunnen and then go
across Schwyz to take me to his castle.

RUODI: Will he be going by the land route then?

TELL: He thinks so.

RUODI: Hide yourself then. Right away.
God will not help you twice out of his hand.

TELL: Tell me the nearest way to Arth and Kuessnacht.

RUODI: The open road will take you over Steinen,
but there's a shorter, and a secret way
the boy can take you, leading over Lowerz.

TELL: (*Gives him his hand.*)
God will reward this deed. Now fare you well.
(*Going, he turns.*)
Didn't you swear your oath, back at the Ruetli?
I'm sure somebody told me –

RUODI: I was there,
and swore the oath of the confederacy.

TELL: Do me the favour of hurrying to Buerglen,
my wife will be despairing of me, tell her
that I am safe, and being well looked after.

RUODI: Where shall I tell her you have fled to, though?

TELL: You'll find my father-in-law with her, and others
who took their oaths together at the Ruetli –
tell them to be of good heart and courageous,
say Tell is free and has his weapon with him,
and they will soon be hearing news of me.

RUODI: What have you got in mind? So tell me freely.

TELL: Once it is done, it will be talked about. (*Goes out.*)

RUODI: Show him the way, Jenni – God preserve him!
  What he has undertaken, he will do. (*Goes out.*)

Scene 2

Great Hall at Attinghausen.
The Freiherr ATTINGHAUSEN in an armchair, dying.
WALTER FUERST, STAUFFACHER, MELCHTAL and
BAUMGARTEN are busy about him. WALTHER TELL is
on his knees before the dying man.

WALTHER: It is all over with him. He is gone.
STAUFFACHER: He isn't lying like a dead man –
  look! The feather's stirring at his lips!
  His sleep is peaceful, and his face is smiling.
  (*BAUMGARTEN goes to the door and speaks to somebody.*)
FUERST: (*To BAUMGARTEN.*)
  Who is it?
BAUMGARTEN: (*Coming back.*) It is your daughter, Hedwig.
  She wants to talk to you, to see the boy.
FUERST: (*Standing.*) Can I bring comfort to her? Or myself?
  Must all this suffering mount up on my head?
HEDWIG: (*Pushing her way in.*)
  Where is my child? Let me go, I must –
STAUFFACHER: Control yourself, think, in a house of death –
HEDWIG: (*Falling on the boy.*)
  My Wally! Oh, he is alive!
WALTHER: (*Clinging to her.*)   Oh, Mother!
HEDWIG: But is it true? And you have not been hurt?
  (*Examinees him with anxious care.*)
  And is it possible he could aim at you?
  How could he do it? Oh, he has no heart –
  that he could fire the arrow at his child!
FUERST: He did it in an agony of soul,
  he was forced to do it, it was life or death.
HEDWIG: If he had had a father's heart, he would
  have died a thousand times, before he did it!!
STAUFFACHER: You should praise the hand of Providence,
  which has ordained –

HEDWIG: You think I can forget
    what could have happened? O, dear God almighty!
    If I live to be eighty, I shall see
    him standing there tied up, his father aiming,
    the arrow always flying to my heart.

MELCHTAL: If you knew how the Governor provoked him!

HEDWIG: What is the heart of men? Their pride's insulted,
    they think of nothing else, set on to play,
    with mother's heart and children's heads for counters?

BAUMGARTEN: And is your husband's fate not hard enough,
    that you must make things worse with constant blame?
    Have you no feeling for his suffering?

HEDWIG: (*Turning and fixing him with a look.*)
    Are tears all you have for a friend in danger?
    Where were you when they put that splendid man
    in fetters? Where was your assistance then?
    You looked on, let the dreadful thing take place,
    you patiently allowed them to remove
    your friend from out your midst – had Tell
    ever acted so to you? Did he just stand there, sadly,
    While the Governor's horsemen galloped after you,
    while the boiling waters of the lake began to roar?
    He did not sympathise with idle tears,
    but sprang into the boat and clean forgot
    both wife and children in his bid to save you –

FUERST: What could we have dared to do to save him,
    so few of us, and all of us unarmed ?

HEDWIG: (*Throws herself on his breast.*)
    Oh Father! He is lost to you as well!
    and to the country, and to all of us,
    he is lost to all, as all are lost to him!
    May God preserve his soul from desperation.
    No friendly comfort can break through the walls
    of his dark castle dungeon – if he falls sick!
    Yes, in the damp and darkness of a dungeon
    he must fall sick – as the mountain rose
    grows pale and sickly in the marshy air,
    for him there is no life except in sunlight,

and in the sweet-breathed currents of the air.
A prisoner! Him! His very breath is Freedom.
He cannot live in stenches from the pit.

STAUFFACHER: Calm yourself. All of us wish to act
to open up his prison.

HEDWIG: What can you do without him? As long as he
was free, there was still hope. Innocence had
a friend, the persecuted had a helper.
He rescued all of you, but all of you
cannot together free him from his shackles!
(*The FREIHERR wakes.*)

BAUMGARTEN:
He's moving! Quiet!

ATTINGHAUSEN: Where is he?

STAUFFACHER: Who?

ATTINGHAUSEN: I need him.
and now he leaves me in this final moment.

STAUFFACHER: He means his son, Rudenz – what news of him?

FUERST: He has been sent for – Be you of good comfort!
He's found his heart again, and he is ours.

ATTINGHAUSEN: Did he speak in favour of his fatherland?

STAUFFACHER: Heroically.

ATTINGHAUSEN: But why does he not come,
so that he may receive my final blessing?
I feel my end cannot be long delayed.

STAUFFACHER: That is not so, my Lord. Your recent sleep
has rested you, your eyes are bright again.

ATTINGHAUSEN: Pain is Life, and that has left me too,
suffering is gone, and so has hope.
Who is that boy?

FUERST: Give him your blessing, Sire.
He is my grandson, now left fatherless.
(*HEDWIG, with her son, sinks to her knees before the dying
man.*)

ATTINGHAUSEN: And fatherless is how I leave you all.
Oh, that my last gaze sees my country's ruin!
Have I had to reach life's highest stage
to die, along with everything I'd hoped for?

STAUFFACHER: (*To FUERST.*)

    Is he to leave us in this gloomy way?
    Should we not illuminate his final hour
    with one bright ray of hope? – Noble Freiherr!
    Raise up your spirits! We are not yet quite
    alone, abandoned beyond salvation.

ATTINGHAUSEN: Who is to save you?

FUERST: We ourselves. Now hear!

    The three cantons have passed their solemn word
    they will combine to drive away the tyrant.
    The alliance is concluded, and an oath
    unites us all. We shall negotiate;
    before the new year starts to move along,
    your dust will find peace in a land of Freedom.

ATTINGHAUSEN: Oh, tell me then! The alliance is concluded?

MELCHTAL: On the same day, all three cantons will rise.

    all is prepared, the secret is well kept
    till now, although it's known to several hundred.
    the earth beneath the tyrants' feet is hollow,
    the days of their ascendancy are numbered
    and soon there'll be no trace of them remaining.

ATTINGHAUSEN: What of the strongest castles in the lands?

MELCHTAL: On one and the same day they will all fall.

ATTINGHAUSEN: And do the nobles favour this alliance?

STAUFFACHER:

    Should there be need, we count on their support,
    for now, the countrymen alone have sworn.

ATTINGHAUSEN: (*Rises slowly, in great astonishment.*)

    The countrymen have dared to make this move,
    alone, without the aid of the nobility,
    trusting so much to their own strength – oh, then,
    they do not need us any longer. We
    may now go down into the grave in peace:
    life will go on – it will be other forces
    that will preserve Mankind and give it glory.

    (*He lays his hand on the head of the child, who kneels before him.*)

    From this head, where the apple had been placed,

will grow, for you, the newer, better, freedom:
the old collapses, and the times will change;
a future life will blossom from their ruins.

STAUFFACHER: (*To FUERST.*)
Look at the light that's shining in his eyes!
That can in no sense be the end of Nature,
it is the first ray of a future life.

ATTINGHAUSEN: The nobleman comes down out of his fastness
to swear confederacy with the cities;
in Uechtland, and in Thurgau it has started,
and Berne, the noble, raises her powerful head,
Freiburg is a safe stronghold for free men,
and bustling Zuerich arms her guilds into
a warrior army – and the might of kings
falls down before her everlasting walls –
(*He speaks now in the voice of a prophet – his speech rising to
inspiration.*)
I see the princes and the noblemen
in suits of armour come into the lists
against a humble, peaceful folk of shepherds.
The struggle will be one of life and death;
and passes shall be ennobled by much bloodshed.
A countryman shall bare his breast, and charge,
a ready sacrifice, into the field of lances,
he breaks through them. The flower of chivalry
falls. And in triumph Freedom's flag is flown.
(*Taking hold of the hands of FUERST and STAUFFACHER.*)
So you must hold together – strong, eternal –
no fort of freedom stranger to another –
see you establish lookouts on your mountains,
so that the allies may assemble quickly –
and be in unity – unity – unity –
(*He falls back into the cushions, his dead hands still clasping
those of the others. FUERST and STAUFFACHER look at each
other for a while in silence, then move apart, each a prey to his
own suffering. The servants meanwhile, have entered silently,
and now approach with signs of varying degrees of suffering,*)

219

some kneel in tears, over his hand. During this silent scene the
bells of the castle are sounded.)

RUDENZ: (*Bursting in.*) Is he still alive? Can he still hear me?

FUERST: (*Turning away his face, pointing.*)
You are now our feudal Lord Protector,
this castle now goes by another name.

RUDENZ: (*Seeing the corpse, he stands gripped by violent anguish.*)
Oh, God! Does my repentance come too late?
Could he not have lived a pulse beat longer,
to see the alteration of my heart?
His honest voice, when he was still alive,
was something I despised – now he is gone,
now he is gone for ever, leaving me
this heavy debt unpaid! – oh, let me know –
did he pass on with ill-will towards me?

STAUFFACHER: He heard, just as he died, what you had done
and blessed the courage, with which he heard you'd spoken.

RUDENZ: (*Kneeling by the dead man.*)
You holy relics of an honoured man!
You lifeless body, here I promise you,
here in your cold shroud – I have destroyed
for ever all those foreign ties that held me.
I have been given back to my own people,
I am a Swiss, and that is what I want –
with all my soul. (*Standing.*) We mourn our friend,
the father of us all, but do not weaken!
His property is not all I have inherited:
his heart and spirit have come down to me,
and my young hand shall now perform for you
those things that you still owe his honoured age.
Give me your hand, oh honourable father!
And give me yours! Melchtal, give me yours too!
Oh, have no fears, and do not turn away!
Receive here both my promise and my oath.

FUERST: Give him your hand. His new-converted heart
deserves our trust.

MELCHTAL: Your countrymen you've not considered.
Then tell us what we may expect of you.

220

STAUFFACHER: Your father's last word was to stay together,
    remember that!
MELCHTAL: Then here is my hand!
    A peasant's handshake is a man's sworn word,
    noble sir! What are the gentlefolk without us?
    Our standing is much older than your own.
RUDENZ: I honour it, and ever shall my sword protect it.
MELCHTAL: That arm, Herr Freiherr, that subdues the earth,
    and makes it fruitful, is an arm that can
    shield a man's breast at need.
RUDENZ: And so you shall
    shield mine, and mine will shield your own.
    One strength shall grow the stronger with the other.
    What are we talking for? Our fatherland
    is still a prey to foreign tyranny.
    Once the soil has been cleansed of enemies,
    then we can settle arguments in peace.
    (*After a moment's silence.*)
    You say nothing. Have you nothing to say to me?
    Am I not yet deserving of your trust?
    In that case I must force myself, against
    your will, into the secrets of your league.
    You had convened – and sworn out on the Ruetli –
    I know – know everything you did out there;
    and everything confided in me by
    other men than you, I have kept to me
    as if it was some holy pledge. Believe me,
    I never was an enemy of my country,
    and nor would I have acted against you.
    But you were wrong to let things so delay,
    the hour is late, and speed is sorely needed.
    Tell is already victim of your hesitation.
STAUFFACHER: We had resolved to wait till Christmas.
RUDENZ: I was not there. Nor did I swear an oath.
    Just wait, and I shall act.
MELCHTAL: What? But you wanted –
RUDENZ: As I now count myself among the country's
    Elders, my first duty is to protect you.

FUERST: Your first, indeed your holiest duty is
  to give back to the earth this worthy dust.
RUDENZ: When we have freed this land, then we shall lay
  the wreath of Victory upon his bier.
  O friends! It is not only your affair,
  I have my own to settle with the tyrant –
  my Berta has been secretly abducted,
  boldly, an outrage, taken from our midst!
STAUFFACHER: The Governor dared perform this outrage on
  a member of the free nobility?
RUDENZ: My friends! And I had promised you assistance
  which I must now beg from you for myself.
  The one I love is taken, snatched away,
  and where the maniac is hiding her, who knows?
  Or what foul powers they have employed against her,
  to force her heart to such a loathed alliance!
  Do not abandon me, oh, help me save her!
  She loves you, she deserves it of her country
  that all should take up weapons in her cause –
FUERST: What do you mean to do?
RUDENZ: How do I know?
  In this dark night, that shrouds her fate, and in
  the terrible fear of this uncertainty,
  where I can find no hopeful thing to grasp,
  one thing and one thing only's clear to me:
  only from the ruins of the power
  of the tyrant can she ever be set free.
  We must be sure that every castle falls,
  to see if she is held within its walls.
MELCHTAL: Then lead you on. We'll follow you. Why put
  off till tomorrow what can be done today?
  Tell was still free, when we swore at the Ruetli.
  This terrible thing had not yet taken place.
  The changing times bring changes in the laws,
  who is so cowardly, who still hesitates?
RUDENZ: (*To STAUFFACHER and FUERST.*)
  Meanwhile you wait in arms and readiness
  until the signal fires flame from the mountains,

when, faster than a winged messenger can bring
the news, the tidings of our victory shall reach you.
So when you see the sight of welcome fires
down on the enemy, like lightning strokes,
and in this ruin, tyranny expires.

Scene 3

The narrow street near Kuessnacht.
One comes downstage from the back between rocks. Passers-by
become visible from the top, before they reach the stage. Rocks
border the whole scene, and on one of the rocks in front there is
a platform overgrown with shrubs.

TELL: (*Entering with his crossbow.*)
He has to come along this narrow street,
there is no other way to Kuessnacht – here
I'll make an end – the chance could not be better.
That elderberry bush will hide me from him,
aimed down from here the bolt is sure to hit him,
the narrowness of the path will foil pursuit.
Governor, settle up your bill with Heaven,
for you must leave, your time will soon be up.
My life was quiet and peacable – my shots
were all restricted to the woodland beasts,
my mind did not concern itself with murder –
you it was that scared me from that peace,
transforming all the milk of pious thinking
into a boiling dragon's venom, you
accustomed me to horrors – he who has
found in a child's head a fitting target,
can find another in an enemy's heart.
The wretched, innocent, child, the faithful wife
I had to shield them, Governor, from your rage,
and at that moment, as I wound the string –
as my hand trembled – as your devilish,
cruel enjoyment forced me to take aim
at the child's head – and while I pleaded
powerlessly with you, that was the moment when

223

I swore an fearful oath that only God could hear,
that the first target of my second arrow
should be your heart – and what I promised then,
in that dread instant of infernal pain,
is a holy debt, I'll now pay back again.
You are my Lord, my Emperor's Governor,
and yet the Emperor himself would not
have dared to do what you – he sent you here
into these lands to speak for Law – severe,
for he was angry – but not, with murderous zeal,
freely to indulge all horrors you might find
attractive to your corrupted insolence.
God will avenge and punish arrogance.
Then come to me, you who can bring such grief,
and now the dearest one of my possessions,
I'm giving you a target, that till now
was proof against the weapons of entreaty –
but you it won't withstand – and you, my trusted
bowstring, who have done me such good service
in sport, do not desert me now in earnest.
Now hold fast one more time, you faithful cord,
that added wings so often to my arrows,
for should this now fall powerless from my hand,
I have no second one at my command.
(*People cross the stage above.*)
So I shall sit here on this bench of stone,
erected for the wanderer's brief respite –
for there's no staying here – each traveller
passes the other swiftly, as a stranger,
asking no questions of his joys and woes –
the care-laden business man, the pilgrim
travelling light – the pious monk, the robber
of gloomy looks, the cheerful careless minstrel,
the pedlar with his heavy-laden horse,
who comes here from the distant lands of men,
for all roads lead to the ending of the world.
They all pass by and travel onward, further,
in their affairs – and my affair is murder!

When your father used to leave you, dearest children,
there was the joy of seeing him again
on his return, always bringing something,
some pretty Alpine flower, unusual bird,
some fossil-shell you find upon the mountains –
but now his quarrel has another quarry,
he treads the savage path with murderous thoughts,
it is his enemy's life he lies in wait for.
And yet he only thinks of you, dear children,
yes, even now – how to defend you, and protect
your innocence from the tyrant's vengeful rage.
His bow is strung. In murder he'll engage!
(*He stands.*)
I lie in wait for worthy game – the hunter
must not allow himself to be discouraged
by daylong wandering in the winter's cold,
springing in reckless leaps from rock to rock,
struggling up the smoothest mountain face,
held only by the sticking of dried blood,
for the hunting of some wretched mountain brute.
I hunt here for a more important quarry,
my enemy's heart, which sought to ruin me.
(*Cheerful music heard in the distance, coming nearer.*)
My whole life long, I've exercised the bow,
and practised all the rules of archery,
I often hit the bull's eye, and brought home
a host of prizes from those friendly contests.
Today, though, I must win the master-shot,
bring down the highest prize in all the land.
(*A wedding procession goes across the stage and up the narrow
street. TELL watches it, leaning on his bow. STUESSI, the field
guard, goes over to him.*)
STUESSI: That is Herr Klostermeier from Moerlischachen
that's getting wed there – he's a wealthy man.
He's got at least ten herds up in the mountains.
He's fetched the bride today from Imisee,
and there'll roistering enough tonight.
Come on! The invitation's open to us all!

TELL: A serious face is not best at a wedding.

STUESSI: Forget your sorrows, shake them off your heart!
　　Take what's on offer, nowadays life's hard,
　　and everyone should take what he can get,
　　there's celebrations here and burials elsewhere.

TELL: And often one gets mixed up with the other.

STUESSI: That's how the world goes now. And Heaven knows
　　there's accidents enough. They had a landslide
　　in the Glarner land, and now there's a whole side
　　of Glaernisch disappeared.

TELL: 　　　　　　　　　　　　The mountains too?
　　Is nothing steady left upon this earth?

STUESSI: You hear the strangest things from other places.
　　I spoke to someone who'd arrived from Baden:
　　told me a knight was riding to the King
　　and on the way a swarm of hornets met him
　　which fell upon his horse, and left it dead.
　　The rider made his way to the King on foot.

TELL: Even the weakest of us gets a weapon.
　　(*ARMGARD comes with several children and takes up her
　　position at the opening of the narrow road.*)

STUESSI: Everyone's talking of a national disaster,
　　brought on by crimes committed against Nature.

TELL: But every day that sort of things can happen,
　　it doesn't need to be a premonition.

STUESSI: It's a happy man who owns his land in peace,
　　and sits unharmed, his family at his fireside.

TELL: Even the best of us cannot stay in peace,
　　if his neighbour's ill-will cannot accept it so.
　　(*TELL repeatedly and expectantly glances up at the top of the
　　road.*)

STUESSI: I'll say farewell then – waiting here for someone?

TELL: I am indeed.

STUESSI: 　　　　　　A safe return home then!
　　Are you from Uri? Our lord Governor
　　is expected to get here today from there.

WAYFARER: He won't be coming any more. The waters
　　have overflowed after all that heavy rain,

and all the bridges are unusable.

ARMGARD: (*Coming forward.*)

    The Governor won't be here?

STUESSI: Want him for something?

ARMGARD: Oh yes!

STUESSI: Why do you put yourself here then,

    Right in his way in this closed-off street?

ARMGARD: He can't avoid me here, he'll have to hear me.

FRIESSHARDT: (*Comes hastily down the street and shouts onto*

    the stage.) Clear out of the way there – my lord the Governor

    is close behind me.

ARMGARD: He is coming then!

    (*Goes, with her children to the front of the stage. GESSLER*

    and Rudolf der HARRAS on horseback, appear at the top of

    the street.)

STUESSI: (*To FRIESSHARDT.*)

    How did you manage to get through the water,

    if the current had taken down the bridges?

FRIESSHARDT: Oh Friend, we fought a battle with the lake.

    We aren't afraid of any mountain streams.

STUESSI: You were on board a ship in all that storm?

FRIESSHARDT: That we were. I shan't ever forget it…

STUESSI: Stay, tell us then!

FRIESSHARDT: I must go on ahead,

    I have to announce the Governor in the fortress. (*Exit.*)

STUESSI: Even with good men on the ship, she would

    have foundered, and gone down with all hands on her.

    that bunch can't work with water, nor with fire.

    (*He looks round him.*)

    Where is the huntsman I was talking to?

    (*He goes out. Enter, on horseback, GESSLER and Rudolf der*

    HARRAS.)

GESSLER: Say what you will, I am the Emperor's servant

    and must consider the services I do him.

    He has not sent me to this land to flatter

    or to indulge the people – it's obedience

    he wants: the quarrel is, who is the master

    here in the country? Emperor or peasant?

ARMGARD: Now is the moment! Now I shall approach him!

GESSLER: I did not put the hat up there in Altdorf
    as a joke, nor was it an attempt to test
    the people's hearts, since I already know them.
    The hat was there so they should learn to bow
    their heads to me, they normally keep upright –
    I gave them some discomfort to go past,
    something that they could see and be reminded
    of that most sovereign Lord they were forgetting.

HARRAS: And yet the people do have certain rights –

GESSLER: To consider them is now not the time!
    Affairs of pith and moment are at work,
    the empire will expand; and what the father
    began so gloriously, the son will now complete.
    This little people here is in our way –
    one way or other – they will finally submit.

    (*They make to continue. ARMGARD throws herself down in front of GESSLER.*)

ARMGARD: Mercy, Lord Governor! Mercy, mercy, mercy!

GESSLER: Why are you blocking my way in the open street?
    Get back!

ARMGARD: My husband is in prison, my good Lord,
    his wretched children cry for bread – have mercy,
    mighty Lord, with our distress!

RUDOLF DER HARRAS: Who are you?
    Who is your husband?

ARMGARD: A poor grasscutter,
    noble Sir, from Rigiberge, who
    mows the grass down off the steep mountain walls
    over the precipices, where the sheep and cattle
    do not dare set foot, where they –

HARRAS: (*To GESSLER.*)   By God,
    a dangerous and miserable life!
    I beg you, set him free, the wretched man,
    whatever crime it is that he's committed,
    his dangerous work is punishment enough.
    (*To ARMGARD.*)
    You shall have your legal due – there in the castle

repeat your plea – for this is not the place.

ARMGARD: No, no, I shall not stir a foot from this place,
until the Governor gives me back my husband!
These past six months now he's been in the tower,
waiting in vain for judgment from the courts.

GESSLER: Woman, would you presume to offer violence?
Out of my way!

ARMGARD:　　　　Then give me justice, Governor.
You are the Emperor's representative
and God's. Then do your duty! As you hope
for mercy for yourself, show it to us.

GESSLER: Come, get that insolent drab out of my sight.

ARMGARD: (*Grabbing the bridle of the horse.*)
No! Because I have nothing more to lose,
you do not leave this place, Lord Governor,
until you show me justice! Knit your brows
and roll your eyes all you will – because we are
so measurelessly wretched that your anger
is a matter of indifference to us.

GESSLER: Woman, give way, or I shall ride you down.

ARMGARD: Let it all go over me – there – now I lie here.
(*Pulls her children to the floor and throws herself with them in his way.*)
And so do my poor children. Let them be crushed.
It will not be the worst that you have done.

HARRAS: Woman, are you insane?

ARMGARD: (*With increased violence.*) You trod the Emperor's land
under your feet a long long time ago!
Oh, I am just a woman! If I were
a man, I would know better things to do
than lie here in the dust –
(*The wedding music can be heard again, at the top of the street, but muted.*)

GESSLER:　　　　　　　　Where are my men?
Get them away from up there, or I shall
forget myself, and do something I'll regret.

HARRAS: The men-at-arms cannot get through, my Lord,
the entry has been blocked off by a wedding.

GESSLER: As ruler of these people I am still
    a deal too mild – their tongues are free to speak,
    things are not yet quite under full control –
    but that will soon be changed, I promise you,
    and I shall break this stubborn obstinacy,
    and bend this barefaced fostering of Freedom.
    There will be a new law promulgated
    in this country, and I shall…
    (*An arrow transfixes him, he claps his hand to his heart, speaking
    with a choked voice.*)
                           God have mercy!
HARRAS: Lord Governor – God, what is this? Where was it from?
ARMGARD: (*Flaring up.*)
    Murder! Murder! He stumbles, sinks. He's hit!
    Right in the heart! That's where the arrow got him!
HARRAS: (*Jumping from his horse.*)
    What a dreadful thing – oh God – my Lord
    beg for the mercy of God – you are a man
    about to die!
GESSLER: The arrow's one of Tell's.
    (*Slides off his horse into the arms of Rudolf der HARRAS, and
    is laid down on the bench.*)
TELL: (*Appearing above, on top of a rock.*)
    You know the marksman, do not look for another!
    The huts are free, and innocence is safe
    from you, you can do no more damage here.
    (*He vanishes from above. People stream in.*)
STUESSI: (*Leading.*)
    What's going on? What's is it's happened here?
ARMGARD: The Governor was shot through with an arrow.
PEOPLE: (*Bursting in.*)
    Who's shot?
    (*While the leading people in the bridal procession are on the stage,
    the ones behind are still upstage, and the music continues.*)
HARRAS: Go and get help. And catch the murderer.
    He's bleeding here to death. – Oh, poor, lost man,
    is it to end for you like this?
    You never heeded any of my warnings.

STUESSI: God, look, he's lying there, all pale and lifeless!

PEOPLE: Who did it, then?

HARRAS: Are all these people mad,
To bring music to murder? Silence there!
(*The music stops abruptly, more people come onto the stage.*)
Lord Governor, speak to me, if you can – have you
no more you wish to tell me?
(*GESSLER makes a gesture, repeating it violently, as it has not
been understood.*) I should go where?
To Kuessnacht? – I don't understand – oh, please,
please do not be impatient – leave behind the things of
this world now. Reconcile yourself with Heaven.
(*The wedding party is now grouped round the dying man with
horror but no feeling.*)

STUESSI: Look, he's all pale – now, now, death's getting to
his heart – his eyes have gone.

ARMGARD: (*Lifting up a child.*)
Look, children, look, see how a tyrant dies!

HARRAS: Madwomen! Have you no feelings left at all?
That you can calmly feast your eyes on this?
Help me – give me a hand now – is there no one
will help me pull the arrow from his breast?

WOMEN: (*Stepping back.*)
We should not touch a man whom God struck down!

HARRAS: A curse be on you, and damnation! (*Draws his sword.*)

STUESSI: (*Stays his hand.*) Sire, too daring!
Your power is at an end. The tyrant of
this country is no more. And we do not
accept this further violence. We are free men.

PEOPLE: (*Tumultuous.*)
The land is free.

HARRAS: And have things come so far?
Is fear so quickly over, and obedience?
(*To the MEN-AT-ARMS, who have entered.*)
You see the hideous act of murder that has been
perpetrated here – help is of no avail –
nor is there any purpose to be served
in seeking for the murderer – we are pressed

by other worries – now, form up, for Kuessnacht!
We can preserve the Emperor's stronghold for him!
For in this moment, all the bonds of duty,
all forms of order too, have been dissolved,
and no man's loyalty can still be trusted!
(*As he goes out with the MEN-AT-ARMS, six FRIARS appear.*)

ARMGARD:

Room, there, make way ! There are the Brothers of Mercy.

STUESSI: The sacrifice is there – here come the ravens.

FRIARS: (*Forming a semicircle round the dead man, and singing in deep voices.*)

'Death lies about the ways of men,
no term is set for him to end his strife.
Midway along his road, the last "Amen"
tears him away from in the midst of life.
Prepared or not, at last he stands alone,
to give account before the Judgment Throne.'

End of Act Four.

ACT FIVE

Scene 1

Square in Altdorf.
Stage right, the fortress of Uri, the scaffolding still in position as in Act
One Scene 3. Left, a panorama of mountains, on all of which there are
signal fires burning. It is just daybreak, bells are ringing from various
distances.
RUODI, KUONI, WERNI, MASTER STONEMASON, and many
others, including women and children.

RUODI: You see the fire signals on the mountains?
STONEMASON: And can you hear the bells out over the woods?
RUODI: The enemy is on the run.
STONEMASON: The forts have fallen.
RUODI: And must we here in Uri suffer still
    the presence of the tyrant's castle then?
    Are we the last to say we are free men?
STONEMASON:
    Must we still bear the yoke that makes us slaves?
    Come, down with it!
ALL: Down with it! Down!
RUODI: Where is Uri's herald?
HERALD: Here. What shall I do?
RUODI: Climb to the watch-tower, blow upon your horn
    so that the noise resounds throughout the mountains,
    and, waking every echo in the valleys,
    summons the men of the region here together.
    (*HERALD goes out. FUERST enters.*)
FUERST: Stay! Friends, Stay a moment! We have as yet
    no news of how things stand in Schwyz and Unterwalden.
    Let us wait for their representatives.
RUODI: Wait? What for? The tyrant is now dead.
    This is the dawning of the day of Freedom.
STONEMASON: Are not those flaming messengers enough,
    alight on all the mountains here around us?

RUODI:
Come, all of you, lend your hands, come, men and women,
bring down the scaffolding! The walls – the arches –
no stone here should be left upon another!
STONEMASON:
Comrades, your hands! We put the damned place up,
we don't need telling how to tear it down.
ALL: Come!! Down with it! (etc)
(*They throw themselves onto the building from every side.*)
FUERST: It has begun. I can no longer stop them.
(*MELCHTAL and BAUMGARTEN enter.*)
MELCHTAL: What? Is the fortress standing still, and Sarnen
lies now in ashes, and the Rossberg too?
FUERST: Is that you, Melchtal? Do you bring us freedom?
Is the enemy driven from the land?
MELCHTAL: The floor is swept and clean. Rejoice, then, father!
At this very moment we are talking,
there is no tyrant left in Switzerland.
FUERST: How did you subdue the fortresses?
MELCHTAL: At Sarnen castle it was Rudenz, who
with true heroic daring overcame them,
the night before I'd occupied the Rossberg.
But hear what happened. When we'd chased the enemy
out of the castle, and cheerfully set it ablaze,
the flames were crackling already up to Heaven
when Gessler's servant, Diethelm, suddenly
cried out the Bruneck woman was still inside.
FUERST: Dear God!
MELCHTAL: She had been secretly imprisoned
by order of the Governor. Rudenz rose
in fury – we could hear the beams give way,
and the main pillars, and from the smoke there came
the cries of the unhappy woman.
FUERST: Was she saved?
MELCHTAL: She was. Rudenz and I, the two of us together,
dragged her from the flames, hearing behind us
the beams collapsing – and as soon as she
saw that she had been saved, and raised her eyes

to Heaven, then the Freiherr fell on my breast
and we, in silence, swore a solemn oath
which, tempered in the fire's heat, will stand
the test of any stroke of destiny.

FUERST: And Landenberg, where is he?

MELCHTAL: Over the Bruenig.
I could not suffer him to leave that place
with both his eyes intact, the man who blinded
my father. I pursued him, took him in flight,
and brought him to my father's feet. The sword
was swinging over his head, when, by the mercy
of that blind old man, he begged him for his life,
and it was granted him. On which he swore
an oath of peace, he never would return.
And he will keep it. He has felt our power.

FUERST: Good that you made this victory without bloodshed!

CHILDREN: (*Running across, with pieces of scaffolding.*)
Freedom! Freedom!
(*The horn of Uri blown powerfully.*)

FUERST: This has become a feast-day. Children will
remember this day when they are grandfathers.
(*GIRLS bring in the hat on its pole; the stage fills with people.*)

RUODI: Here is the hat we had to make our bows too.

BAUMGARTEN: Tell us now just what we should do with it.

FUERST: God! It was under that my grandson stood!

SEVERAL VOICES: Destroy the remnants of the tyrant's power!
Into the fire with it!

FUERST: No! preserve it!
It had to be the tool of tyranny,
now it will always be a sign of Freedom!
(*The COUNTRY PEOPLE, men, women and children, stand or sit round the planks of the destroyed scaffolding in a wide semi-circle.*)

MELCHTAL: Now we are standing joyfully upon
the ruined walls of tyranny, it is fulfilled
the things we swore to, comrades, on the Ruetli!

FUERST: The work has been begun, but not yet ended.
    Now we shall need our courage, and our union,
    be not deceived, the King will not delay
    to avenge the death of his late Governor,
    or to bring back those who were driven out.
MELCHTAL: Let him come, with his armies; from the inside
    of the country the enemy is driven out.
    And we shall meet all enemies from the outside.
RUODI: Few passes give an access to this land,
    and we shall close the walls up with our bodies!
BAUMGARTEN: We are bound to one another, as with chains,
    and all his armies shall not make us fear him.
    (*ROESSELMANN and STAUFFACHER enter.*)
ROESSELMANN: It is a fearful judgment from above.
PEOPLE: What is it?
ROESSELMANN: What times we live in!
FUERST: Say, what is it?
    Ha, is it you, Herr Werner? What do you bring us?
PEOPLE: What is it, then?
ROESSELMANN: Listen and be astonished!
STAUFFACHER: From one great terror we have just been freed –
ROESSELMANN:
    The Emperor has been murdered.
FUERST: God in Heaven!
    (*The people all rise and crowd round STAUFFACHER.*)
PEOPLE: Murdered? The Emperor? What? Listen! The Emperor?
MELCHTAL: Impossible! Where did you get this news?
STAUFFACHER:
    It's true enough. At Bruegg the Emperor Albrecht
    fell to the murderer's hand – a man, whom I believe,
    Johannes Mueller, brought it from Schauffhausen.
FUERST: Who was it dared to do this dreadful thing?
STAUFFACHER: The perpetrator makes it still more dreadful.
    It was his nephew, his own brother's child,
    Duke Johannes of Swabia, who did it.
FUERST: But what brought him to parricide?
STAUFFACHER: The Emperor
    withheld the inheritance from his father

from the impatient creditor: it was said
he intended to deprive him entirely,
buying the boy off with a bishop's mitre.
However that may be – the boy gave ear
to his brothers-in-arms and their seditious talk,
and with the noblemen von Eschenbach,
von Tegerfelden, von der Wart and Palm,
he decided, since he could not hope for justice,
he would pursue a judgement on his own.

FUERST: Tell me though, how was the crime accomplished?

STAUFFACHER: The King was riding down from Stein zu Baden
towards Rheinfelden, where the court was held.
With him the Princes Hans and Leopold,
along with a train of high-born gentlemen.
As they came to the Reuss, which one must cross
by ferry, the murderers pressed into the ship,
separating the Emperor from his retinue.
Then, as the Emperor rode across a field –
beneath which lies an ancient city from
heathen times – opposite him the fortress
of Hapsburg, whence his family's grandeur issued –
Duke Hans there drew his dagger through his throat,
Rudolf von Palm, with his spear, ran him through,
while Eschenbach then split his head in two,
so that he sank down, drenched in his own blood,
murdered by his own vassals, on his own land.
Those on the opposite bank all witnessed this,
but, cut off by the river, they could not do
more than send up a powerless cry of woe.
But by the wayside there was a poor woman,
and in her lap the Emperor bled to death.

MELCHTAL: So he has hollowed out his early grave,
whose greed for everything could know no limits!

STAUFFACHER: A dreadful fear has shaken all the land,
all of the mountain passes have been blocked,
all territories are looking to their frontiers,
even old Zuerich has locked up her gates
which had been standing open thirty years,

fearing the murderers and, still more, the avengers.
For now, armed with the curse of jurisdiction, comes
the Queen of Hungary, the fierce Agnes,
quite unacquainted with the mildness of
her gentle sex, to avenge her father's blood
on his murderers' servants, children, grandchildren,
indeed the very stones of their castles' walls.
She swore to send whole generations down
into her father's grave, then, as she's said,
'to bathe in blood, as if in Maytime dew'.

MELCHTHAL: Do they know where the murderers have fled to?

STAUFFACHER: They fled away as soon as the deed was done
in five completely different directions
and separated, never to meet again –
Duke Johann's said to be wandering in the mountains.

FUERST: So shall their misdeed never bear them fruit!
Vengeance does not bear fruit! For she herself
is the appalling nourishment, whose taste
is murder, and whose satisfaction, horror.

STAUFFACHER: The crime will bring no profit to the murderers;
we, however, come with clean hands to pick
the blessed fruit of bloody sacrilege.
For we have been released from one great fear:
the enemy of Liberty is gone,
and, as announced, the sceptre shall now pass
from Hapsburg's house to some other line.
The Empire shall preserve freedom of choice.

FUERST / OTHERS: Have you heard anything?

STAUFFACHER: The majority
already voted for the Count of Luxemburg.

FUERST: Happily we stayed loyal to the Empire;
now there is hope for justice in this land!

STAUFFACHER:
He'll badly need brave friends, the coming Master,
he'll shield us from the Austrians' revenge.
(*The countrymen embrace one another. Enter PETERMANN*
the sexton with an IMPERIAL MESSENGER.)

PETERMANN: Here are the region's high authorities.

ROESSELMANN / OTHERS:

   What is it, Sexton?

SEXTON: An imperial messenger brings this letter.

TUTTI: Break the seal, read it!

FUERST: (*Reading.*)   'To the loyal men

   of Uri, Schwyz and Unterwalden, Queen

   Elizabeth here offers grace and all good wishes.'

SEVERAL VOICES:

   What does the Queen want now her rule is over?

FUERST: (*Reading.*) 'In her great sorrow and viduity

   occasioned by the bloodthirsty demise

   of her husband, Her Majesty thinks once more

   of the old devotion and fidelity

   of the Swiss provinces.'

MELCHTHAL: She never gave a thought to it before.

ROESSELMANN: Silence! Let's hear it!

FUERST: (*Reading.*) 'And she expects from her most loyal subjects

   that they shall hold in most especial horror

   the accursed perpetrators of this deed.

   She will expect therefore from the three provinces

   that they give no assistance to the murderers,

   rather that they will readily assist

   in the deliverance of them to their avengers,

   mindful of the love and ancient favour

   that they have long enjoyed from the house of Habsburg.'

   (*Signs of dissatisfaction among the COUNTRYMEN.*)

VOICES: Love and Favour?!

STAUFFACHER: Such favour as we had was from the father;

   what gratitude, though, do we owe the son?

   Has he confirmed the letters of agreement,

   which every Emperor has done before him?

   Has he judged after the ancient code of justice,

   protected persecuted innocence?

   Has he even listened to the envoys

   who we had sent to him in our distress?

   Not one of all these things has he performed

   for us, and had we not created our own right,

   with our brave hands, our need would not have touched him.

239

Thank him?! He sowed no thanks here in these valleys.
He stood in state, the highest in the land,
he could have been a father to his people,
but he was pleased to look after his own,
and prosper them. Well, now let them mourn him!
FUERST: We shall not be rejoicing at his fall,
nor shall we commemorate the evil done,
far be it from us! But that we should avenge
the death of one who never did us good,
pursuing those who never did us harm,
that is no business nor concern of ours.
Love should mean voluntary sacrifice:
Death looses all the chains of duty forced,
for him we've nothing further to discharge.
MELCHTHAL: And as the Queen sheds tears up in her chamber,
and flings her accusations against Heaven,
the people you see here are free from fear,
they send their thanks to that same Heaven above –
those who would harvest tears, must first sow Love.
(*IMPERIAL MESSENGER leaves.*)
STAUFFACHER: (*To the people.*)
But where is Tell? Shall he alone be wanting,
the author of our freedom? It was he
who did the most, who passed the hardest trial.
Come, in procession to his house, and call
Hail to the Saviour, Saviour of us all!

Scene 2

*TELL's house. A fire in the chimney. The door stands open to
the outside.*
HEDWIG, WALTHER and WILHELM.

HEDWIG: Your father's back today. Oh, my dear children!
He's free, alive, and so are we, and all!
And yes, it was your father saved the country!
WALTHER: And I was there too, Mother, don't forget
to mention me as well! When Father's arrow
just grazed my life, I didn't even tremble!

HEDWIG: (*Embracing him.*)

    Yes, you've been given back to me! Twice now

    I've given birth to you, twice known the pains

    of motherhood for you! But it's over now –

    I've got the two of you, the two of you!

    And soon, today, I'll have your father back!

    (*A MONK appears in the doorway.*)

WILHELM: Look, Mother, look – there is a holy brother,

    he's sure to want some charity from us.

HEDWIG: Go, bring him in. We'll give him some refreshment.

    He must have felt the atmosphere in here.

    (*Goes indoors and returns with a jug.*)

WILHELM: (*To the MONK.*)

    Come in, good father. My mother wants you to.

WALTER: Come in and rest, until you've got your strength up.

MONK: (*Timidly looking round, his features distraught.*)

    Where am I? Tell me, what land am I in?

WALTHER: Lost your way, have you? That why you don't know?

    You are in Buerglen, Sir, in Canton Uri,

    the entrance to the valley of the Scaechen.

MONK: (*To HEDWIG, who is coming back in.*)

    Are you alone? Or is your husband here?

HEDWIG: I'm waiting for him now – but what is it, man?

    You do not look as if you brought good news.

    Whoever you are, you need to eat and drink!

    (*Hands him the beaker.*)

MONK: However much my thirsting heart may long

    for comfort, I'll not touch it till you promise –

HEDWIG: Do not touch my dress, and stay away

    from me, if you wish me to listen to you.

MONK: I swear, by that hospitably burning fire,

    by these dear children's heads, that I now grasp –

    (*He grabs hold of the children.*)

HEDWIG: Man, what are you thinking of? Get back!

    let go of my children! You are not a monk!

    You are not! Peace dwells in such a habit,

    there is no trace of such things in your face.

MONK: I am the most miserable of men.

HEDWIG: Unhappiness speaks strongly to the heart,
  but in your eyes there's something chills my soul.
WALTHER: (*Jumping up.*)
  Mother, it's Father! (*Dashes out.*)
HEDWIG: Oh, my God!
  (*Wants to follow, but trembles and stops short.*)
WILHELM: (*Hurrying after his brother.*) Father!
WALTHER: (*Off.*) You're back again!
WILHELM: (*Off.*)   Oh, Father, welcome home!
TELL: (*Off.*) Here I am back again. Where is your mother?
  (*They come in.*)
WALTHER: She's standing at the door and can't get further,
  she's trembling for fear and happiness!
TELL: Oh, Hedwig, Hedwig, mother of my children!
  God gave His aid – no tyrant can divide us now.
HEDWIG: (*Arms round his neck.*)
  Tell ! Tell! The fear I have been in for you!
  (*MONK becomes noticeable.*)
TELL: Forget it now. We'll have nothing but joy.
  I'm back again! I'm standing in my house!
WALTHER: But where's your crossbow, Father? I don't see it.
TELL: Nor will you see it, son, not any more,
  from now it's kept safe in a holy place,
  I shall not use it for the hunt again.
HEDWIG: (*Stepping back, letting go his hand.*)
  O Tell, Tell!
TELL: Why are you frightened, dearest wife?
HEDWIG: What – how have you come back to me – your hand –
  am I to take it? – this your hand – oh God!
TELL: This hand defended you and saved the country,
  I may now hold it up to Heaven in freedom.
  (*The MONK makes a sudden movement, TELL notices him.*)
  Who is the brother there?
HEDWIG: Oh, I forgot him!
  Can you speak to him, he gives me the horrors.
MONK: (*Approaching.*)
  Then are you Tell, the man who killed the Governor?
TELL: Yes, I am he, I hide the fact from no one.

242

MONK: So you are Tell! It was the hand of God
   that led me here, to come under your roof.
TELL: (*Examining him closely.*)
   You're not a monk. Who are you?
MONK: You have killed
   the Governor, who did you harm – I too
   have slain an enemy who refused me justice.
   He was your enemy as well as mine –
   I freed the country from him.
TELL: (*Recoiling.*)   Then you are –
   oh horror! – Children, children run on in.
   Go, dearest wife! Just go! – Unhappy man,
   then you are –
HEDWIG: God, who is it?
TELL: Do not ask!
   Go! Now! Go! The children must not hear.
   Just leave the house – go far away – you cannot
   be under the same roof as this man here.
HEDWIG: Oh God what is this? Come along!
   (*Leaves with the children.*)
TELL: (*To the MONK.*) You are the Duke of Swabia – you are!
   You killed the Emperor, your Lord, your uncle.
PARRICIDA: He robbed me of my just inheritance.
TELL: You killed your uncle and your Emperor!
   And does the earth still bear you, does the sun
   still shine on you?
PARRICIDA: Tell, listen to me, before you –
TELL: You dare to come here, dripping with the blood
   of parricide, of regicide, and set foot
   inside my guiltless house, and show your face
   to an honest man, expecting hospitality?
PARRICIDA: I hoped to find some mercy from a man
   who also took his vengeance on his enemy.
TELL: Do you confuse ambition's bloody guilt
   with the self-defending actions of a father?
   Did you preserve your children's heads, defend
   the sanctity of your home? Or keep away
   the last, most dreadful things from what you loved?

I raise a pair of guiltless hands to Heaven
and I curse you and what you did – I have
avenged the holy nature you defiled –
nothing do I have in common with you:
you did murder, I preserved what I held dear.

PARRICIDA: Then you reject me, comfortless, in despair?

TELL: It makes my flesh creep just to speak with you.
Go! And pursue your horrifying path,
keep from the huts, where innocence still lives.

PARRICIDA: (*Turning to go.*)
I can no longer live like that, nor will I !

TELL: And yet I pity you your – God in Heaven!
So young, of such impeccable descent,
grandson of Rudolf, of my Lord, my Emperor,
and now a murderer and a fugitive,
here at my door, the poor man's door, despairing –

PARRICIDA: If you can weep, let my condition move you,
for it is truly terrible – I am
a prince – I was – I could well have been happy
if I had stemmed the impatience of desire.
But Envy gnawed my heart away – I saw
the young days of my cousin Leopold
crowned with honour and paid with land, while I
who was the selfsame age as he, was kept
in a slave-like inferiority.

TELL: Unhappy man, your uncle knew you well
to keep you from controlling land or people!
Your hasty, savage act of madness gives
justification to his wise decision.
Where are the bloody henchmen of your murder?

PARRICIDA:
Gone where the avenging spirits may have led them.
I have not seen them since the crime was done.

TELL: You know the ban of outlawry pursues you,
forbidden your friends, but open to your foes?

PARRICIDA: So I avoid the open streets, and do
not dare to knock at the meanest hovel's door.
It is to the desert I direct my feet.

I wander, like a horror through the mountains,
recoiling from myself if I should see
my miserable reflection in a stream.
If you have mercy, or humanity –
(*Falls down before TELL.*)
TELL: (*Turning away.*)   Get up ! Get up!
PARRICIDA: Not until you give your hand to help me.
TELL: How can I help you? Can a man help sin?
    Stand up – however terrible the thing
    that you have done – you are a man – as I am –
    I send no man away without some comfort –
    whatever I can do, I'll do.
PARRICIDA: (*Jumping up and violently gripping his hand.*)
                         Oh, Tell!
    You save my soul from final desperation.
TELL: Let go my hand – you must leave here. You cannot
    stay here unknown, once known you cannot count
    on safety – where do you mean to go – and where
    do you hope to find peace?
PARRICIDA: How do I know that?
TELL: Listen to what God tells me in my heart –
    you go to Italy, to St Peter's city;
    throw yourself at the Holy Father's feet,
    confess your guilt, and so redeem your soul.
PARRICIDA: Will he not hand me over to the avengers?
TELL: What ever he does, accept it as God's will.
PARRICIDA: How do I get into this unknown land?
    I do not know the way, and do not dare
    to attach myself to any other pilgrims.
TELL: I shall tell you the way, just listen well!
    You start to climb against the current of
    the Reuss, where its wild stream bursts from the mountain –
PARRICIDA: (*In fear.*)
    I'd see the Reuss? It flowed then, past my crime.
TELL: The way leads down and down, and many crosses
    have been put up, erected to the memory
    of wayfarers whom the avalanche has buried.

PARRICIDA: I do not fear the violence of Nature,
 if I can tame the wild storms of the heart.
TELL: Fall down in front of every cross in penance,
 atoning for your guilt in tears of rue –
 once you are lucky to be past the gorge,
 providing the mountain sends no further snow
 down on you from the ice-covered ridge,
 then you will come to the bridge, the Bridge of Spray.
 If it will bear the weight of your great guilt,
 once you have happily left it behind you,
 a black rock face will rear up, never yet
 illumined by a ray of daylight – you go through it,
 it leads you into a bright and peaceful valley –
 but you will need to hasten through at speed,
 you may not tarry in a place of rest.
PARRICIDA: Oh, Rudolf, Rudolf, oh, my royal uncle!
 This is your grandson's entry to your kingdom!
TELL: Then keep on climbing, and you reach the heights
 of the St Gotthard, where the eternal lakes are,
 that fill themselves with water from the heavens.
 There you will say farewell to German lands,
 another river, the Ticino, takes you
 happily into Italy, for you the Promised Land.
 (*The 'Ranz des Vaches' is heard, played on several alpine horns.*)
 I can hear voices. Go!
HEDWIG: (*Hurrying in.*) Where are you, Tell?
 Your father's coming! The confederates
 are all in a procession –
PARRICIDA: Oh, my God!
 I cannot show my face among the happy.
TELL: Go, dearest wife and give this man to eat
 and drink, and everything he heeds, the way
 he goes is long, and he will not find shelter.
 Hurry! They're here!
HEDWIG: Who is it?
TELL: Ask no questions!
 And when he leaves, just turn your eyes away

so that you do not see the way he goes!

(*PARRICIDA makes a quick move towards TELL, who raises a hand to put him off, and goes. When they have both left in different directions, the scene changes.*)

Final Scene

The land in front of TELL's house, and the nearby heights which surround it, are crowded with people. Others are arriving over a high walkway, leading over the river Schaechen. WALTER FUERST with the two boys, MELCHTHAL and STAUFFACHER come forwards, others pressing behind them; as TELL comes out all receive him with loud cheers.

TUTTI: Hurray for Tell, our saviour and protector!
(*While those in front crowd around TELL and embrace him, RUDENZ and BERTA appear, he embracing people in the crowd, she embracing HEDWIG. This wordless scene is accompanied by the music from the mountain, When this comes to an end, BERTA steps into the middle of scene.*)
BERTA: Countrymen! And confederates ! Accept me
in your alliance, the first happy woman
to find protection in the land of Freedom!
In your brave hands I here do lay my rights,
will you accept me as a citizen?
TUTTI: We will!
BERTA: My hand to this young man I dedicate.
A free Swiss woman takes a free Swiss man.
RUDENZ: From this day forth my serfs I liberate.
(*As the music quickly strikes up again, the curtain falls.*)

The End.

Also in this series

Schiller: Volume One
The Robbers / Passion and Politics
Translated by Robert David MacDonald
9781840026184

Schiller: Volume Two
Don Carlos / Mary Stuart
Translated by Robert David MacDonald
9781840026191